THE ABIDING PRESENCE

COMMUNION MEDITATIONS

Other Books by William Powell Tuck

Facing Grief and Death
The Struggle For Meaning (editor)
Knowing God: Religious Knowledge in the Theology
    of John Baillie
Our Baptist Tradition
Ministry: An Ecumenical Challenge (editor)
Getting Past the Pain
A Glorious Vision
The Bible As Our Guide For Spiritual Growth (editor)
Authentic Evangelism
The Lord's Prayer Today
The Way for All Seasons
Through the Eyes of a Child
Christmas Is for the Young...Whatever Their Age
Love as a Way of Living
The Compelling Faces of Jesus
The Left Behind Fantasy
The Ten Commandments: Their Meaning Today
Facing Life's Ups and Downs
The Church In Today's World
The Church Under the Cross
Modern Shapers of Baptist Thought in America
The Journey to the Undiscovered Country:
    What's Beyond Death?
A Pastor Preaching: Toward a Theology of the Proclaimed Word
The Pulpit Ministry of the Pastors of River Road Church, Baptist
    (editor)
The Last Words from the Cross
Lord, I Keep Getting a Busy Signal: Reaching for a
    Better Spiritual Connection
Overcoming Sermon Block: The Preacher's Workshop
A Revolutionary Gospel: Salvation in the Theology of
    Walter Rauschenbusch
Holidays, Holy Days and Special Days
A Positive Word for Christian Lamenting: Funeral Homilies
Star Thrower: A Pastor's Handbook
A Pastoral Prophet: Sermons and Prayers of Wayne Oates (editor)

THE ABIDING PRESENCE

COMMUNION MEDITATIONS

William Powell Tuck

CSS Publishing Company
Lima, Ohio

THE ABIDING PRESENCE

FIRST EDITION
Copyright © 2017
by CSS Publishing Co., Inc.

Published by CSS Publishing Company, Inc., Lima, Ohio 45807. All rights reserved. No part of this publication may be reproduced in any manner whatsoever without the prior permission of the publisher, except in the case of brief quotations embodied in critical articles and reviews. Inquiries should be addressed to: CSS Publishing Company, Inc., Permissions Department, 5450 N. Dixie Highway, Lima, Ohio 45807.

Library of Congress Cataloging-in-Publication Data
Names: Tuck, William Powell, 1934- author.
Title: The abiding presence : communion meditations / William Powell Tuck.
Description: Lima, Ohio : CSS Publishing Company, Inc., 2017.
Identifiers: LCCN 2017009721 | ISBN 9780788029011 (pbk. : alk. paper) | ISBN 0788029010 (pbk. : alk. paper)
Subjects: LCSH: Lord's Supper--Meditations.
Classification: LCC BV826.5 .T83 2017 | DDC 264/.36--dc23
LC record available at https://lccn.loc.gov/2017009721

For more information about CSS Publishing Company resources, visit our website at www.csspub.com, email us at csr@csspub.com, or call (800) 241-4056.

e-book:
ISBN-13: 978-0-7880-2902-8
ISBN-10: 0-7880-2902-9

ISBN-13: 978-0-7880-2901-1
ISBN-10: 0-7880-2901-0   PRINTED IN USA

Contents

	Preface	9
1.	Holy Communion	13
2.	In the Breaking of Bread	21
3.	The Communion Cup	31
4.	A Meal That Lasts	41
5.	On Being Unworthy	49
6.	A Reminder in Your Hand	59
7.	Learning To Eat At The Lord's Table	67
8.	A Time For Celebration	75
9.	The New Covenant	83
10.	Communion In A Time Of Survival	93
11.	A Christmas Eve Communion Meditation	103
12.	The Abiding Presence	113

To my
Ph.D. and Th.M. graduate students
at
The Southern Baptist Theological Seminary
Doug Dortch, Ronald Hinson, Jr., Joel Snider
and
Edward Culpepper, David Hull, Lee McGlone,
Ronald Poythress and Keith Stuart
and
Doctor of Ministry students at
The Southern Baptist Theological Seminary
and
The Baptist Theological Seminary at Richmond

Preface

The observance of the Lord's Supper is one of the most significant events in the worship of the Church. It is observed in various ways and at various times. Some congregations observe communion every Sunday, like the Disciples of Christ, while others observe it monthly or quarterly. The Roman Catholic Churches not only have communion on Sundays but daily. Many congregations often observe communion on special church days like Maundy Thursday. In some congregations, the communion elements are received in the pew as the congregation kneels on the kneeling pad in front of them. Other congregations have the participants come forward and either kneel at an altar railing or stand to receive them at the front from the minister or priest. In many congregations, the communion trays are passed down the aisles as the congregation serves themselves from the trays that are passed.

Some argue that communion is restricted to a worship setting in church. Some others claim that the Lord's Supper is a "movable feast" and can be observed in the home, hospital, nursing home, on a college campus, in retreat settings, or in other words anywhere. Others believe that it is restricted to the chancel with a priest officiating. Some congregations allow anyone to officiate; while others affirmed that only ordained clergy can officiate. Most congregations believe that baptized believers should be the participants who receive the communion elements. In some denominations, like the Catholics, with their understanding that only properly baptized believers can take the elements and that only an ordained priest can officiate, have continued to cause division at the communion altar. I personally believe that the division of the church at the table of our Lord is one of the tragedies of the church today. Rather than signifying the church's unity, this disunity at the table has to represent a sad indictment of the church from our Lord's perspective who prayed for its unity.

As we gather at the Lord's table, we always have to remember that it is not our table but the Lord's table. He is the host at the table and we come at his invitation, and we come to observe the *"Lord's"* Supper. Let's pray and work together to bring about the unity of the church, and let us strive to make this unity visible at the Lord's table.

Through the centuries, the church has used various names for the Lord's Supper. I will mention a few of the prominent ones here. One of the earliest designations for the Lord's Supper has been "communion" which was derived from 1 Corinthians 10:16: "The cup of blessing which we bless, is it not the communion (*koinonia*) of the blood of Christ? The bread which we break, is it not the communion of the body of Christ?" Another term drawn from the Corinthian passage is "commemoration" or "memorial." "This do in remembrance of me." (1 Corinthians 11:24). Another name associated with the Lord's Supper is "covenant." "This cup is the new *covenant* in my blood." (1 Corinthians 11:35).

Among the early names for the Lord's Supper was Eucharist which comes from the Greek word for thanksgiving. "The Lord Jesus on the same night in which he was betrayed took bread; and when he had given *thanks*, he broke it." (1 Corinthians 11: 23-24). A name which has been associated with the Lord's Supper in the Eastern and

Roman Catholic traditions is the mass. This name likely is derived from the fourth or fifth centuries from the words used by the priest at the conclusion of the service when he would say in Latin: *"Ite missa est."* "Go, you are dismissed" or often *"missa."* *Missa* in its common form became "mass." The name sacrament was derived from the Roman military oath or pledges which a solider took and became associated with the Christian's commitment or pledge of complete loyalty to Christ. Some traditions prefer ordinance rather than sacrament, but there is no reason that sacrament cannot be a legitimate term when one affirms its significance as a tangible sign or testimony to the consecration of a believer's life to Christ, the central figure at the table, who cleanses him or her from sins. An early name for the Lord's Supper was sacrifice. The original meal Jesus had with his disciples was the Passover which depicted Israel's redemption from Egypt. The Lord's Supper was a depiction of the sacrifice Jesus made for us on the cross which Jesus declared was seen in the broken bread and wine. "For as often as you eat this bread and drink the cup, you proclaim the Lord's death until he comes." (1 Corinthians 11: 26).

What takes place at the Lord's table, in my opinion, is more than merely symbolic. The bread and cup symbolize — represent — depict the sacrificial death of Christ on the cross for us. What happens at this table is an "acted parable" — "a dramatic representation or symbolism" of the atoning sacrifice of Christ. The table cannot be limited to a memorial — a looking back — but is a testimony to the reality of the living presence of Christ with us at the table. We gather at the Lord's table to celebrate the abiding presence of Christ with us today. We do not simply focus on a memory of a dead Jesus but our focal point is on the resurrected Christ who lives and is ever present with us today. Jesus is present at the table and not so much on it or in the elements. He is a teal presence at the table and in our midst today. We gather at the Lord's table to celebrate that abiding presence. Christ is present in the present moment.

These communion meditations were preached at various times in churches where I served as pastor or as an interim pastor. They are one minister's effort to address the wonder of the Lord's table. The meditations based on the biblical passages about the Lord's Supper offer endless possibilities for proclaiming the Good News. The Lord's table may afford us an occasion to speak in a symbolic way that surpasses what we can say with words alone. I want to thank my friend and fellow minister, Rand Forder, for his careful proofreading of the original manuscripts.

1. Holy Communion

Isaiah 53:5-6
1 Corinthians 10:16-17

I have to confess that when I was a teenager I really did not like communion services in my church because it usually told me several things. Number one, it was going to be a long service. Number two, the sermon would have absolutely nothing to do with the communion service. As a teenager, I didn't have the foggiest notion what the service meant. And like many other people, I did not worship well after twelve o'clock. The worship service always· seemed to go beyond twelve when we had Communion, and the observance was always tacked on at the end. Frankly, I could not understand it.

I must also confess that even as a young preacher, and later as a pastor of a country church, I still didn't like communion services very much. I felt that if I had a word from the Lord, a prophetic word that needed to be shared, and the communion service sometime seemed to get in the way of that prophetic utterance. Time, age, study, and participation in communion services have enabled me to capture a different perspective altogether.

The Biblical Roots of Communion

One of the things which I have discovered is that when we share at the Lord's table, we are going back to the *very* foundation of the early church itself. The early Christians often gathered at the table in communion and fellowship together. In Paul's Corinthian epistle, he writes about the cup of blessing which was the third cup in the Passover meal of the Jewish people. The cup of blessing was a special blessing for the wine cup which was to follow. Paul, drawing on that figure, moves on to remind the church that the cup of blessing in which we share is communion with the blood of Christ. "Is the bread in which we share," he asked, "not communion with the body of Christ?"

The word, communion, is *koinonia*, a very familiar Greek word to many of us today. It. is often translated communion. At the very heart of one of the few sayings in the New Testament concerning the Lord's Supper, the word "communion" itself is used. It has always hit me in a rather ironic way that many Baptists do not like the word, yet "communion" is a very biblical word

In fact, "communion" is the word which Paul uses on a number of occasions to describe what we do when we gather at the Lord's table. It is a "communion" — a fellowship. Unfortunately, many of us think of fellowship as primarily sitting around drinking coffee together, or having a piece of pie or cake or engaging in some kind of recreational activity.

But in this letter Paul is talking about fellowship — "communion." When we participate in the body and blood of Christ in this way at his table, we are identifying with him. We are communing with him. This reference goes back to what Paul saw happening all around him. In this passage from 1 Corinthians, Paul is struggling with the whole question of eating food offered to idols. One of the concerns that Paul raised here is whenever one ate any food that had been placed on the sacrificial altar to another god, he or she was in a way identifying with that god. When the Jewish people shared in the paschal lamb at the Passover feast, they were sharing in and communing with the God of the Exodus whom they attempted to worship. So then, we commune with Christ when we partake of the cup and the bread. They unite us in fellowship with him and with one another.

The Greek word "communion" has been translated in various' ways. In the *Revised Standard Version* it is translated as "participation" or "partaking." In the *New English Bible*" It is rendered "sharing." Do we not share in the blood of Christ? Do we not share in the body of Christ? We share in his body as we are recipients and receive what he has done for us. The suffering servant image from the great Isaiah depicts one who has laid down his life for us; one who was bruised by our iniquities; and as the one who has borne the chastisement of our sins. We share in what he has done for us as we receive it; and we identify with him in his suffering as we give our life to him in service.

Passing on the Experience of Christ

We are to share further not only as we receive but as Christians we commune with others. We commune and share when we also pass on the love which we have experienced in Christ. We pass on and share with others what we have experienced in his forgiving, loving, redeeming grace. We have shared in it as we have communed with Christ and now we share his love with others.

Living a Redemptive Life

But go now even further with me. Knowing that we have shared in Christ's presence with us at the Lord's table, and we have identified our lives with his life, we now share that life as we go into a world to live differently because of this relationship. Having shared at his table, having communed with him, having experienced anew the power of his grace, and having experienced again the awesome power of that redemptive love, we now live differently because of our experience with him. There are things that we no longer seek to do. We avoid the ways of sin. Thorvaldsen, the noted Danish sculpturist, was asked if he would accept a commission to carve a statue of the goddess Venus. Thorvaldsen said: "The hand that carved the form of Christ can never carve the form of a heathen goddess." Having sat in communion with Christ, our lives are enriched by the power of his living presence. His presence is supposed to make us radically different. He gives us a new birth, a new commandment, a new song, a new life, and new hope. We cannot live now as though we have not experienced redeeming powerful grace.

The Sense of Mystery at the Table

As I have grown older and wiser, I come to the table aware of the great mystery that surrounds this time of togetherness at Christ's table. I am aware that none of my feeble words, or anyone's words, or the greatest declarations by the most profound theologians can ever capture fully what the death, sacrifice, and resurrection of Jesus Christ mean. Our words are always inadequate. Our words always ring hollow when we try to proclaim what God has done for us in Jesus Christ. We pause between our words, searching and groping to find ways to explain what the death of Christ really means.

When I was a student in seminary, I took a semester course in the doctrine of the atonement. We studied various theories about the death of Christ. We examined his death as sacrifice, ransom, propitiation and many other theories. We read noted theologians and New Testament scholars, but there was no way, even in after having read all of these great minds and in searching through the scriptures to understand the meaning of the death of Christ, could any of us fully put its meaning into words. All we can do is we simply proclaim the mystery of what God has done for us through Christ.

A Time of Holiness

As we commune at Christ's table, this becomes for us a time of holiness. The word' "holy" literally means "set apart." We come setting apart this time, this place, this table, and ourselves. We set apart the elements, the wine and the bread, as symbols of the presence of Christ at his table. He is the one who is ultimately set apart so he can make his way to come among us. We set ourselves apart that we might experience his presence with us.

The word communion and the word common come from the same Greek root. The elements which we use in the Lord's Supper are common elements — bread and wine, from grain and grapes. They are common ingredients of life. We gather now as ordinary people to commune at his table and to use common elements that are set apart in some feeble attempt to talk about the mystery of God's love. We acknowledge the mystery of the sacrificial death of Christ and proclaim loudly and clearly that there is never anyone who fully understands it or can explain it so that we are totally satisfied. The one person you and I should not listen to is the one who thinks he or she can explain the mystery. We gather at this table to acknowledge the mystery and we take off our shoes because we know we are on holy ground. Moses realized he was on holy ground when he stood before the burning bush. Isaiah knew he was in the presence of the Holy One when he had a vision of God high and lifted up. We come to his table with a sense of the holiness and mystery of God which goes beyond our words to describe it.

A Community of Faith

The words communion and community are linked together also in their roots. We gather as a community of faith to share at Christ's table and to express our fellowship one with the other. We share the love of Christ. We share the message of the love of Christ with others. As you and I gather in a congregational setting, I learned a long time ago that people do not have to listen when I preach. They can pretend that they are listening while they think about everything else. We are all masters at tuning people out both here and in other places. Persons in church on Sunday morning do not have to sing. I wish they would sing, and I wish they would listen. When the communion trays are passed in church or one is invited to come forward and receive communion, you do not have to share in the communion service, but you must make a decision whether to participate or not to participate. As the elements are thrust into your hand, they demand from you a decision. You must decide whether or not you will share in the mystery of the cup of Christ and the bread of the body of Christ. If a person sees you across the street, you can ignore them if you want to. When that person comes across the street and thrusts his hand into yours and seeks to shake hands with you, then you must make a decision whether you will shake his hand or not. Now you must decide about communion.

In a few moments the cup and the bread will be passed into your presence. I am hoping, as a part of the body of Christ in this community which links its hands with Christians around the world, that each of us might sense something of the great mystery of the presence of the living Christ. Come now to the table of the Lord. I invite all Christians to share with us as we commune at Christ's table. We come at his invitation because it is his table. I invite all to sup with him and with each other as we sense his Spirit among us.

Lord, we open our hearts to commune with Your Spirit now.

2. In the Breaking of Bread

Exodus 12:30-34
John 6:33-35
1 Corinthians 13:23-24

We have all seen the swollen stomachs, bulging eyes and thin bodies of small children who are starving. These images haunt and disturb us. The Food and Agriculture Organization (FAO) reports that 858 million people around the world are suffering from chronic hunger. Natural disasters and wars are an impetus for famine, hunger and poverty and are a serious threat for world peace and security. Our own country has its pockets of hunger, deprivation and poverty. Most of us present today have likely never experienced real hunger like being on the verge of literally starving to death.

In Jesus' day many people lived on the edge of starvation. They normally ate two small meals a day and rarely ate meat. There were no fast food stores or grocery stores to purchase bread or other items. When Jesus taught his disciples to pray, "Give us this day our daily bread," they understood that prayer request as a serious one. They understood what it meant to say that "bread is the staff of life." His listeners would have also understood the story about the prodigal son who wasted all his inheritance in riotous living and became so hungry that he would have gladly eaten the pods of the unclean swine he was now feeding. Hunger was a familiar companion then.

Broken Bread

Bread was also a familiar part of the religious life of the people of Israel. Their major religious celebration, The Passover, gave bread a significant role. Three unleavened loaves was placed on the table in front of the host for the celebration of the meal. The unleavened bread was a reminder of the haste the Children of Israel left Egypt without having time for the bread to leaven. At a point in the Passover meal, the host would take one of the loaves and break it into small pieces. The broken pieces were to remind them of the affliction they suffered in Egypt, and that a slave never had a whole loaf to eat but only pieces. The host would then say: "This is the bread of affliction which our forefathers ate in the land of Egypt. Whosoever is hungry, let him come and eat; whosoever is in need, let him come and eat the Passover with us." Following this, it was the duty of the father to explain what the Passover meal meant. The youngest child would ask: "Why is this night different from other nights?" And then the father would share the story of their deliverance from Egypt and the Passover which God provided for them.

His Body

When Jesus gathered in the upper room with his disciples to celebrate the Passover meal, he took a loaf of bread, and after giving thanks, he broke it and said: "This is my body that is for you. Do this in remembrance of me" (1 Cor. 13: 24). The disciples must have been shocked by those words. Jesus was asking them not to remember the exodus, but him. Here was the foretelling of his sacrificial death on the cross. The bread, he declared, represented his body. The Greek word for body in the New Testament is *soma*, and the medical term *psychosomatic* is drawn from that root word and expanded to encompass mind and spirit. The biblical concept of body denoted flesh and spirit — the totality of our being. Jesus' reference to body, I believe, is also an attestation to his incarnation. "The word became flesh — a human being — and lived among us" John wrote in his prologue (John 1: 14). The incarnation is about the unique entrance of the divine spirit into humanity — the Word became flesh — body. Jesus' reference to the bread as his body is a summons for us to remember the mystery of the grand miracle of the Christian faith, the incarnation.

The Real Presence

Following the feeding of the five-thousand, the crowd of people he had just fed demanded that Jesus give them a sign that he could continue to supply them bread. He then tells them, "Very truly, I tell you, unless you eat the flesh of the Son of Man and drink his blood, you have no life in you. Those who eat my flesh and drink my blood have eternal life; and I will raise them up on the last day" (John 6: 53-54). His listeners did not grasp the meaning of what Jesus was saying and were in fact scandalized by them. No Jew would eat flesh or drink blood.

Some people today attempt to take these words of Jesus literally and believe that the bread and wine literally become his body and blood again at the Eucharist. This is the complicated belief called transubstantiation. This they see it as the "real presence" of Christ in the Lord's Supper. I believe in the real presence of Christ *at* the table but not on it or in the elements. The bread and wine, as Jesus himself declared, are in remembrance of him and are not in actuality him. As we gather at the table, we do not commune with a memory or a symbol but with a real person, the living Christ. The risen Christ is the real presence at the communion table not the elements that direct us to that presence. His spiritual presence as the risen, living Lord is the One we encounter at his table.

Known in the Breaking of Bread

Following the crucifixion of Jesus, two believers were traveling on the road from Jerusalem toward Emmaus and were discouraged and despondent. Suddenly a stranger appeared and joined them in their journey and conversation. He inquired why they all were so despondent, and they asked if he is not aware of what happened to Jesus in Jerusalem who was arrested and put to death. They said that they had high hopes that he was the Messiah. The stranger then began to expound the scriptures from Moses to the prophets and showed from them how the Messiah was to be arrested, beaten and crucified. When they arrived at the journey's end, the two travelers invited the stranger to have a meal with them. At the table the stranger took bread, blessed it and broke it, and gave it to them. "Then their eyes were opened and they recognized him (Jesus); and he vanished from their sight" (Luke 24: 31). When they recognized Jesus, their "hearts burned within them," and they immediately rose that same hour and returned to Jerusalem. The risen Christ was made known to them in the breaking of the bread.

As we gather at the communion table, is it not our desire that we, too, might recognize the living Lord in the breaking of the bread? The reality of the risen Christ is the ground-bed of our faith. Recently I visited in the home of a family for whom I was conducting the funeral service for their mother who had died suddenly at eighty-three. As I sat in the living room talking to them about the service and their mother's religious faith, I noticed the painting above some of the family members who were sitting on the sofa. I learned that it had been painted by the deceased mother's sister. It was a painting of Jesus walking with one of the men on the Emmaus Road after his resurrection. I, of course, made reference in my funeral meditation to this painting of the Emmaus Road. It was a commanding affirmation of the assurance of the risen Christ; and likewise it affirms our hope in life beyond the grave for those who trust in the risen Christ. The communion table affords us a special worship opportunity to commune with the spiritual presence of the living Christ.

The Real Bread

A popular tradition among the Jewish people was that before the new age dawned, a prophet like Moses or Elijah would appear at Passover and feed Israel as Moses had fed them in the wilderness. After feeding the five thousand people, the crowd wanted to know if Jesus would give them another miracle as Moses did to "prove" he was the Messiah. Jesus told them that it was not Moses who fed the Israelites in the wilderness but God. He declared that "my Father" was the source of the bread not Moses; and God gives the true bread from heaven. The people then asked: "Sir, give us this bread always." Then Jesus boldly exclaimed, "I am the Bread of Life" (John 6: 35)..."I am the living bread that came down from heaven. Whoever eats of this bread will live forever; and the bread that I will give for the life of the world is my flesh" (John 6: 51). In my opinion this passage is misunderstood when one tries to take this declaration of Jesus literally. This is one of John's seven "signs' that point beyond the physical to the spiritual reality in revealing truth about Christ and the Kingdom of God. Ordinary bread points to bread, the One who is the real bread, the true bread, the living bread — Jesus Christ.

I believe that even the request for "our daily bread" in the Lord's Prayer is more than asking for daily physical nourishment but is a reminder of the "manna" that we will share at the heavenly banquet with the Bread of Life in our eternal home. When we share in our ordinary meal every day, cannot our everyday bread help us focus on the true Bread of Life? Christ as the Bread of Life is the one through whom God revealed the divine presence in the fullest sense. Through Christ, God's spirit sustains us, feeds us, nourishes us, and guides us into authentic living. At the Lord's table, we seek to draw near to the one who is the alpha and the omega, the beginning and the end, the eternal one. He is still prophet, priest and king. As prophet, he calls us to be spokespersons for the least and the needy in our world. As priest, he summons us to love God with our mind, soul, body and strength. As king, he calls upon us to seek first the kingdom of God in all our endeavors.

The bread broken at the table reminds us that Christ was broken for us in his suffering and death on the cross. Just as the bread at the Passover meal was broken into many small pieces reminding Israel of its struggles in their bondage in Egypt, the bread broken at the Lord's table reminds us of the depth of Christ's sacrifice for us on the cross. At the table, we remember that sacrifice but "see" him now as the living, active, vital, perpetual holy redeemer.

Christ Is Host

Christ is the host and central figure at the communion table, not a priest, a pastor or anyone else. It is the "*Lord's*" table. When Leonardo da Vinci was painting what later became his masterpiece of "The Lord's Supper" on the north wall of the little refectory of a convent in Milan, Italy, a friend looking at the painting remarked to him about the brilliancy of the silver cup. Immediately Da Vinci took his brush and painted the cup out of the picture. He was not going to have anything in his picture which drew attention away from the central figure of Jesus. We gather at the table to focus on the central figure — Jesus Christ. We commune with his spiritual presence, not a memory or a symbol.

Take Eat This Bread

Paul reminded his readers, "For as often as you eat this bread and drink the cup, you proclaim the Lord's death until he comes again" (1 Cor. 11:26). Eating the bread and drinking the cup are testimonies to the redeeming sacrifice of Christ and our identity with him. John records Jesus saying in the synagogue at Capernaum, "Those who eat my flesh and drink my blood abide in me, and I in them… This is the bread that came down from heaven, not like that which your ancestors ate and they died. But the one who eats this bread will live forever" (John 6: 56 and 58). The hearers that day found this a "hard saying" and difficult to understand. Some of those who heard this teaching were offended and no longer followed Jesus (John 6:60-66).

This statement of Jesus will continue to offend listeners today if they try to take it literally. The words that refer to eating his flesh and drinking his blood are, in my interpretation, references to his incarnation and sacrificial death on the cross. Referring to the bread at the Passover meal, Jesus declared, "This is my body that is for you" (1 Cor. 11:24). "To eat" Christ is to assimilate his spiritual presence and take him into our inmost being. Just as physical food cannot nourish us unless we eat it and it is taken into our body, Christ cannot impact us unless we assimilate, incorporate, absorb, and take in his spirit, life, and teachings. We eat the Bread of Life to find life. We eat the bread of the spirit to nourish our souls. We eat the bread from heaven to identity with the kingdom of God. Our flesh has to respond to the one who became flesh — a human being in the incarnation. When I was in England several years ago, I had the opportunity to go into the chapel at Keble College, Oxford and see Holman Hunt's original painting of Jesus with a lantern in his hand standing at a large wooden door and knocking. It is obvious that there is no latch on the outside of the door. The door has to be opened from the inside. The message is clear. If we want Christ to come into our lives, we must open from within. We have to respond and assimilate his presence. When the communion bread comes to us, we have to respond to the one who is the Bread of Life and eat the bread as a sign of our allowing Christ to come into our lives.

Eating Bread to Live Forever

As the Bread of Life, Jesus declares that he came down from heaven and "whoever eats of this bread will live forever, and the bread that I will give for the life of the world is my flesh" (John 6:51). This is clearly a reference to his atoning death on the cross. Those who trust in the risen Christ will share in the eternal life we receive in him. We gather at the Lord's table to affirm our belief in the living Lord and the eternal life he bestows on his believers. The broken bread points to the bread of heaven — the Bread of Life.

Robert Morgan relates an account of a visit by the

Methodist Bishop Kenneth Goodson and a religious news editor for the *Birmingham News* with John Lincoln Brasher, a pioneer preacher in Alabama on his one-hundredth birthday. The reporter was spellbound by the conversation with Dr. Brasher, and asked one more question as they were leaving. "Dr. Bratcher, how long do you plan to live?" The old preacher stood erect, leaning on his staff and responded: "How long am I going to live? Forever, Sir! Forever!" The next Sunday was Easter and the lead editorial in the *Birmingham News* on that Easter Sunday read: "Forever, Sir! Forever!"[1]

As we gather at the communion table and eat the bread and drink the cup, we boldly declare that through faith in Jesus Christ, the Bread of Life, we will live forever. Come eat this bread and live.

O Bread of Life, feed us with Your abiding presence.
May Your presence fill us with spiritual nourishment
to love and serve You more effectively.

---

1 Robert C. Morgan, *Who's Coming to Dinner?* (Nashville: Abingdon Press, 1992), 94-95.

3. The Communion Cup

Psalm 116:12-14
I Corinthians 11:23-26

Cups play a prominent part in our lives. We use them to drink coffee, tea, juice, milk, or other liquids. Many of us still have the cup we had as a child, or we have our own children's cups, or our grandchildren's cups. We hang on to them as a way of remembering a special time in the past. I went into a former church member's home, and noticed that a whole wall was covered with shelves displaying various kinds of cups in multicolor. Some people collect cups or mugs that have pictures of various states, countries, colleges or universities, or clubs to which they belong. The Rotary Club, of which I was a member, used to give a cup to its speakers. It was a way of saying thank you to them, and was also a continuous reminder to that individual about rotary.

I had a friend in seminary that always drank his coffee out of the same green cup. I often wondered if he ever washed that cup, because it always seemed to be in use. Many of us have a favorite cup, or mug, that we use for our special beverage.

The Importance of the Cup

The gospels tell us that Jesus took a cup in the Last Supper, and he blessed it. This cup was a part of Jesus' last supper as he celebrated the Passover with his disciples. Some early Christians claimed to have possessed the cup that Jesus used at the Last Supper. They called it the Holy Grail. Stories and miracles were centered on this particular cup for many years. A contemporary writer, Thomas B. Costain, wrote a novel which I read as a teenager, entitled *The Silver Chalice*. This novel was built around the cup of Jesus, how it made its way to Antioch, and the lives that it touched.

The Cup in the Bible

In the Bible, the cup is a reference to the common drinking utensil which often played an uncommon role in the lives of people. For example, there is a cup in the dream of Pharaoh's butler. Joseph interpreted this dream for the butler. Joseph had a cup hidden in his brother, Benjamin's, grain sack as he and his family left to go back home. Through this entrapment, Joseph later revealed to his brothers who he really was. At the Last Supper, Jesus took a cup, and blessed it as a part of the Passover Feast. That cup has continued to be a part of the tradition of the Lord's Supper to this day.

The cup in the Bible is also symbolic in many ways. Some places in the Bible refer to "the cup of bitterness," "the cup of agony," and, "the cup that overflows," which the writer of the twenty-third Psalm noted. Think with me about some of these symbolic cups to which the scriptures refer.

The Cup of Salvation

There is, first of all, the *cup of salvation*. The Psalmist wrote about this cup in Psalm 116. The Psalmist says that, "I will lift up a cup of salvation and call on the name of the Lord." Through the death of Jesus Christ, this cup is offered to all persons. It overflows with the bounty of

God's love, grace, and abundance. The salvation from this cup has overflowed and run down through the centuries until you and I can drink of that cup today.

My wife, Emily, and I had the privilege of attending the Baptist World Alliance meeting in South Africa in 1998. The Africans have many dialects. It is often difficult to translate the biblical images into the African dialect. I heard how the word "salvation" was translated in an interesting way. They translated the word "salvation" with a phrase, "He took our necks out." This phrase had a special meaning to people in South Africa. Captured slaves would be marched in route to the coast to get on slave ships. The slaves had iron collars around their necks, with a chain binding the slave in front of a person to the one behind him, and on down the line. If a person saw a friend or relative among the slaves as they were being marched to the ship, that person could pay the price for the slave and the master would unlock the iron collar, then take the man's neck out and set him free.

"He took their necks out," was a symbolic expression to the African people about God's redeeming grace. They remembered well what it was like to be a slave set free. This image helped them to see that they were set free from the shackles of sin which had bound them. God's grace had freed them and given them new opportunities to live.

Annie Dillard, in her book *Pilgrim at Tinker Creek*, reminds us of the vastness and wonder of God's grace and love when she exclaims, "Experiencing the present, truly, is being emptied and hollowed; you catch grace as a man fills his cup under a waterfall." God's grace is so marvelous and abundant that it is impossible to contain it. Like a person standing with a cup under a waterfall, there is no way that the cup can contain all of the wonder that comes from God's love. God's salvation is beyond our understanding. It is abundant and free.

The Cup of the New Covenant

Second, as we come to the communion table, let us also be reminded of the *cup of the new covenant*. Jesus shared the Passover meal with his disciples, and then lifted his cup to proclaim the beginning of a new era. The cup of blessing was traditionally the last thing at this sacred meal. With his cup raised high, Jesus declared that this "cup was a sign of the new covenant." He had established a new relationship with his disciples. The old Sinai covenant, which was built on the sacrifice of animals, was over.

The covenant was one of the great Old Testament images. It appears many times from Genesis 17 to Revelation 21. A covenant was made with Abraham, and with Moses at Mount Sinai. The covenant God made with Israel was often broken by them, and reaffirmed by God. Jeremiah promised that a new covenant would come, and this covenant would be a law written within their hearts.

Jesus declared that he had established a new covenant by his blood. The disciples, who were Jewish, would not literally want to drink blood. Jesus was saying that his death was a sign, a symbol of the outpouring of life and the creating of a new relationship with God.

Today, we can relate to God differently, because Jesus Christ has made this way to God possible for us. His new covenant was the one which Jeremiah said would be written on our hearts. The cup is a sign of the new covenant, a new relationship with God, brought about by Jesus Christ.

Recently, a young couple stood before me in the sacred place of our church, and they pledged a covenant to each other. This covenant was based on faith, hope, and love — faith in each other, and faith in God; hope in the dreams that they had for their married life, and hope in the presence of God; in the love that they shared for each other, the love of their parents for them, and, most of all, the love of God. It was a covenant in which they bound themselves to each other and to God. Today, we reaffirm, each time we drink the cup of the Lord's Supper, that we are part of the new covenant which Jesus Christ created by his love and sacrifice.

The Cup of Suffering

Third, there is also the *cup of suffering*. As Jesus bowed in agony in the Garden of Gethsemane, he prayed, "Oh Father, if it is possible, let this cup pass from me." What cup? Was it the cup of suffering, the cup of agony, and the cup of death? The mother of two of Jesus' disciples said to him, "Lord, let my sons have the chief seats in your kingdom." Jesus asked them, "Are you able to drink of the cup that I must drink?" They said, "Yes, Lord." But, they really did not know what it was. "Are you able to drink the cup of suffering and agony that I must bear?" Jesus asks us. It is easy to say yes when we really do not know if we can.

The Lord's Supper was instituted within a context of suffering. Jesus knew that he was soon to be betrayed, and that he faced the agony of the cross. Are we able to share in his suffering, to be his instruments to reach out in love to others and touch them? We are challenged by Paul to be ministers of reconciliation — to share the suffering of Christ. Are we able to do that?

I heard about an elderly preacher who was addicted to alcohol, obviously not a Baptist minister. He would do fine for a while, but then, he would begin to drink again. When he did, he lost favor with his family, church, and his bishop. When he was sober, he was always a very pious and upright minister. There was always one individual, a young pastor, who came to his assistance whenever he was in trouble. This young pastor had the reputation of not giving up on people. After a short period of success, and many second chances, the old minister began to drink again. This time, the church would take it no longer, and he was forced to surrender his ordination certificates.

The young minister did not hear about it for some time. When he learned about it, he remembered that the old preacher had a little family farm he would normally go to in times like this. He got in his car and went searching for the farm. When he arrived, he was greeted by the grateful wife of the minister. She told him that the old preacher saw him driving up, and went and hid in the barn. The young minister walked out to the barn and found the old preacher huddled in a corner.

The old preacher cursed him, and said, "I can't stand you, but I knew you would be the only one to come. Thank God, you never let me go." This young minister understood the Gospel message that you should never let anybody go. The good news is that God cares about every single person, no matter what his or her sin is and pursues us like a "hound from heaven" with unconditional love. The young minister suffered with his brother, and brought to him the ministry of reconciliation. As Christians, we are called to reach out with love and concern to others.

The Cup of Consolation

In Jeremiah 16:7, the ancient prophet refers to "the cup of consolation" which was the cup usually given, according to the Jewish custom, to the grieving family at the conclusion of a mourning feast. The community would gather to comfort the mourners and support them in their grief. They would "weep with those who wept." All Saints Day in many Christian churches is the occasion where Christians pause to remember their fellow Christians who have died and have gone to their heavenly reward. Candles and special prayers are voiced for the families of those who have lost loved ones — Christians during the past year. Barbara Crooker has offered her All Saints prayer in these words:

Day of the Dead
November 1st, the veil thinner, and we remember
those who've gone to the other side. Don't worry,
I say, I'll be there soon. But for now, I mark the presence
of their absence, an ache in the throat, a finger
on memory's pulse. Light candles to keep out the dark,
to mark a path, should they wish to return. The floating world
shimmers and ebbs. I'd like to cross over, just for one hour,
see my mother, hold my baby, talk to Clare. Perched on our shoulders,
the dead ride with us, teetering like pyramids of water
skiers, forming enormous wings. Their words, though,
remain inaudible. Cold syllables. They scratch maps in
frost on dark windows, but no one can read them.

Cross the threshold. This night is ancient and long.
Whisper in my ear,
tell me what the new year will bring. Look at how the
candle uses up
its wax. See how the smoke rises in the hearth.[2]

The Cup of Service

Finally, the cup is also symbolic of the *cup of service*. Do you remember that Jesus told his disciples that, "As often as you give a cup of cold water in my name, you minister to me"? All the other cups, the cup of salvation, the cup of suffering, and the cup of the new covenant, lead us to the awareness that, having received such great love, we now are challenged to manifest compassion, mercy, and love, through our lives. Our Lord reached out to the needy and hurting, and he has commissioned us to share the cup of compassion with them. We, who have been reconciled by God, reach out to bring reconciliation to others through God's love and grace.

We are now offered Jesus' cup each time we come to the communion table. As we drink of that cup, our challenge is now to go into the world and to share the love of God with others, so they, too, might drink from his cup. His cup is one of service — self-giving love. To drink of Jesus' cup challenges us to be a part of the redemptive force in the world. We share Christ's cup only as we are his instruments in ministry in the world. Whenever we give "a cup of cold water" to someone in need, we serve our Lord.

When I visited an elderly woman in the hospital who was a member at my former church, I embraced her as I was leaving. She said, "Thank you for doing that, nobody

2 Barbara Crooker, "Day of the Dead," *The Christian Century*, (October 28, 2015), 28.

ever hugs me anymore." There are a lot of people who are waiting for somebody to reach out and embrace them — to share love, to share a touch, to share hope, or to share opportunities. May you and I be God's instruments to others as we lift up the cup of service.

Zollene Reissner, the church organist at one of the churches where I was a pastor, went on a European concert tour with the St. Alban's Choir several years ago. One of the numbers they sang was composed by Petr Eben, a world-renowned Czech composer. He drew his music from the setting of a poem by Delores Dufner, OSB, a member of the Benedictine Community in St. Joseph, Minnesota. It is entitled *From Life to Life*.

O wheat whose crushing was for bread,
O bread whose breaking is for life,
O life, your seeming end is seed,
a seed for wheat, or bread and life.

O fruit whose crushing was for wine,
O wine whose flowing is for blood,
O blood, your pouring out is life,
our life in you, O fruitful vine.

O life whose crushing was for love,
O love whose spending was to death,
O death, your mourning is our joy,
full joy and birth to lasting life.[3]

As you eat the bread at the communion table, reflect

---

[3] Delores Dufner, "From Life to Life," *Wonder, Love and Praise: A Supplement to the Hymnal, 1982*, John L. Hester, editor (New York, NY: Church Publications, Inc., 1997), #760

on the fact that Christ is the Bread of Life. As you drink the cup, remember that Jesus Christ is the one in whom you have life. As you drink, remember the cup of salvation. Remember the Christ, who has suffered, died and has given us salvation. Reflect on the cup of suffering. Remember that you are united to Christ through the cup of the new covenant. When you have finished eating his bread, and sharing his cup, remember you now go to bear the cup of service, in His name, into the world.

Holy God, we cannot fully express our thanksgiving for Your great love, which we have seen through the death of Your son, Jesus Christ. We come, now, to commune at Your table. May we sense Your presence as we approach this moment, in the name of Christ. Amen.

4. A Meal That Lasts

Psalm 51: 10-17
John 6:30-40, 48-51

We are all familiar with the expression, in fact sometime or another we may have said it ourselves, but it is true of children and especially of teenagers. They finish a meal and declare, "I am still hungry!" We all understand that sometimes we do not seem to get enough to eat. We eat a meal, and it is not long before we are hungry again. We all normally eat several meals a day. We long for some food that lasts.

If you recall the story in the Gospel of John, Jesus had just performed a miracle in which he had fed five thousand men, women, and children. The people were deeply impressed by someone who could feed them. So the Scribes and the Pharisees came to him and said, "You have done this wonderful thing. Let us see if you can do something more spectacular. If so, we will know that you really are from God. Prove to us that you are God's chosen one." In the light of this story, think with me about communion around several themes.

Show Us You Are from God

The first lesson we note in our text is the demand that Jesus prove God's existence in his life. That is what the Scribes and Pharisees were asking Jesus. "Prove to us that you are from God." We have seen that kind of question was raised in many places in the gospels. Thomas, for example, was the one who said, "Lord, show us the Father and we will believe." Jesus said, "Thomas, have I been with you so long, and yet you have not seen the Father?" Jesus was saying, "I give evidence of the realness of the Father through my teachings and ministry."

In one of our children's Sunday School classes several years ago, some of the boys and girls were asking their Sunday School teacher a similar question, "How can we know that God is real?" That is the same old issue, "Prove to us that there is a God." Prove God!

What Sign Would You Accept?

What sign would it take to convince you that God is real? Look around you at this fantastic, unbelievable universe! That is a pretty good sign of God. Did the universe just happen? There are some who say that it just happened. To me it takes far more faith to believe that the world just happened by chance, than to say there was a source called God behind it as Creator. What sign would you accept? Would you accept the sign of a hand, suddenly appearing and writing across the sky saying, "I am alive, I am real. Signed, God?" Would that convince you that there is a God? Or, would you think that some preachers have cooked up a scheme to convince you? We search for signs.

Jesus as the Central Sign

Jesus said to the scribes and Pharisees, "You want me to produce bread like Moses produced in the wilderness? Hey, you are wrong. Moses did not give you bread. That bread came from God." Bread was only symbolic of the power of God. This whole universe, and you and I, are symbols, or signs, of the reality of the presence of God. Jesus was saying to them, "I am *the* central sign of the 'realness' of God. When you see me, you know the realness of God. I am the one who makes God real." We can point to Jesus and his life, death, teachings and resurrection to affirm that God is real.

A Bountiful Meal

As we gather at this table, remember also that the Lord's Supper is a plentiful meal. Plentiful! We know all about meals that are bountiful, don't we? I remember when I was a pastor of my church in northern Virginia while I was a student at the University of Richmond. I was one of those starving college students then. You know that it seemed like people were right when they said, "Bill seems to have hollow legs. He could never be filled up." I remember how wonderful it was to go to my church, and then have an invitation to eat at one of the homes in that farming country. When I sat down at their table we would usually have several meats, all kinds of fresh or canned or frozen vegetables from their own gardens and several kinds of desserts to finish the meal. I could never seem to get enough to eat until then. I was always full after those Sunday dinners!

On the third Sunday in August and even to this day, my church, Good Hope Baptist, had and still have their annual homecoming. The tables were stretched out across the lawn with food piled high from all of those families. If you could not get plenty to eat that Sunday, you never could. We all know what it is like at Christmas and Thanksgiving to eat bountiful meals. We eat far more than we can begin to hold. Often our family, after eating a big Christmastime dinner, find ourselves lying around like the Culhaines family in the old TV show. We are so full, we cannot move. We have eaten too much. We understand what it is to eat plenty.

Jesus Is the Bread that Nourishes Us

Yet, some say, "How can this meal at the Lord's table be plentiful? How can this tiny piece of bread and this cup be a plentiful meal?" The bountifulness that the Lord's Supper offers is not a physical replenishment. The Lord's Supper is plentiful, because it reminds us that the presence of Christ as the "Bread of Life" sustains us. The bread and cup remind us that we receive the presence of Christ at the table in a unique way. The bread and cup remind us of the living, risen Christ who is always with us and that we are "fed" by his spiritual presence. He is "bread" not in a way to satisfy our physical hunger, but he gratifies a deeper, spiritual hunger. The elements at the table remind us that we are nourished by Christ and sustained by the one who is the Lord of life. He is the one who revealed to us the sacrificial and unconditional love of God through his life, teachings, miracles, death and resurrection. He has shown us the depth of true living and the meaning of life. He declares, "I am the Bread of Life and when you eat this bread you will not be hungry or thirsty again."

The Lord's Table Is Open to All

Remember as we gather at the Lord's table, there is always room for others. There is always room for another chair to be pulled up. The table of the Lord is never too full that another person cannot come and eat there. That is one of the great universal messages in the Gospel — whosoever will — may come and can be saved by God's grace and be fed at his table.

A pastor in Maine tells about a YMCA basketball league that was active in his community. The YMCA had a policy that every player on the team had to get a chance to play sometime during the season. The coaches could not just let the players sit on the bench. It was the last game of the season. The team that was in first place was playing the team that was in last place. The teams reached the last four minutes of the game and the coaches started substituting players.

The coach of the losing team sent a boy into the game. It did not take long to realize that this boy was not only slow physically, but was a little slow mentally. The players would be going down the court one way, and he would be going the other way. Then they would go the opposite way and he would go the other way. It was obvious after a few times up and down the court that this boy was not completely like the other boys.

Finally, as this lad got in tune with his team and was coming down the court the same way they were. His team had the ball. By accident, one of his players threw him the ball. The whole gym hushed. The officials froze. Everybody stopped and looked at the little lad. The boy stood there with the ball in his hands a moment, turned the ball in his hands a couple of times, took two or three steps without dribbling, and then, shot. The opposing team that had kept their opponents to no more than thirty points in a game did not even raise their hands. They just stood there motionless. The ball hit the backboard and bounced off. A player caught it and threw it to the same boy again.

The boy looked at the ball, took two or three steps without dribbling, and then shot again. The ball hit the rim and went in! A roar went up. The place went wild with yelling. There wasn't a dry eye in the gym. The referees blew their whistles and the coaches substituted again. The boy went back to his bench elated.

The game continued to the end. But that day on a basketball court, a barrier had been broken. The players showed acceptance of someone who was different. They paused, and even broke the rules, so that he might be a part of their group. He went back to his bench, a lad who had probably been the butt of many jokes and the victim of a lot of teasing and harassment, feeling encouraged and accepted by his peers.

When we come to the Lord's table, the good news is that there is a chair for everyone to come and eat of the plenty of God's redeeming grace. No one is excluded. God's loving, forgiving, accepting grace is extended to all who will come.

A Perpetual Presence

Then remember, we come to the Lord's table aware that we are acknowledging food that is perpetual. The bread and cup are lasting in their effect. When we eat of this bread and drink of this cup, we are taking in spiritual nourishment. It is a kind of nourishment which is the very Lord's presence. Some people stumble over the words of Jesus, "You have to eat my flesh, and drink my blood," because they want to take these words literally. But they are metaphors, of course. We use metaphors all the time about drinking and eating. For example, we say: we are drinking in someone's actions or we are devouring a book or we are taking in a show or drinking in a musical CD or tape or I cannot swallow some story or he has ingested his account or she gulped down her feelings or he is consumed by ambition... all of these are only figures of speech.

Open Ourselves to Christ's Presence

By this image, Jesus is telling us that we have to take his presence into ourselves. Accepting him is an individual act, as individual as eating. No one else can eat for you, so no one else can give you the presence of Christ. You have to open yourself and accept him. You can have a room filled with books, but if you do not take one off the shelf and read it, it is not part of you. You may have every CD imaginable, but if you never play one and listen to it, you cannot drink in that music. You may have a wonderful five course meal set before you, but if you do not eat it, it will not nourish you nor will you enjoy it.

So it is with the power of Christ. Christ nourishes you only as you allow him to come into your life and give you his presence. When you do that, you are satisfied. You are satisfied by the power and presence of a Christ that is perpetual. Christ continues to be there, to sustain you in all of your life. Jesus is telling us that the bread he gives is eternal, because it comes with the love, grace, and power of God's presence in and with us. Jesus Christ is the one who is life — life everlasting.

Some of you remember and likely witnessed, and others have read about or seen versions of the event, that in July of 1969, Apollo 11 took off for the moon. One of the persons who was a part of that flight was Buzz Aldrin. He was a devout Christian, a Presbyterian. He talked with his pastor about something he wanted to do on that mission and wondered if it would be acceptable. He wondered if it would be okay to take communion on the moon. The Presbyterian synod gave him permission.

At a certain point after they landed on the moon, the public heard these words as Buzz Aldrin radioed Houston, "This is Eagle. I would like to request a few moments of silence. I would like to invite each person listening in, wherever and whomever he may be, to contemplate for a moment the events of this past few hours and give thanks in his own individual way."

Just imagine, this rocket ship had just landed on the moon for the first time! Buzz said that during this time there was a radio blackout and only silence. During these moments, he took out the plastic package he had taken with him that contained the bread and wine. He said, "I poured the wine into the chalice that our church had given me. With the one-sixth gravity on the moon, the wine curled slowly and gracefully up the side of the cup. It was an interesting thing that the very first liquid ever poured on the moon, and the first food ever eaten there, were communion elements." Communion elements were the first fluid and the first food on the moon!

He continued, "As I partook of the elements I knew my church back home was having communion at the same time as I was. I sensed, especially strong, my unity with our church back home, and with the church everywhere." Then he read this passage of scripture that he had brought, "I am the vine, you are the branches. Whoever remains in me, and I in him, will bear much fruit; for you can do nothing without me." (John 15:5 TEV).[4]

Whether it is on the moon, whether it is here on earth, in Richmond, some remote place across this earth, or even on some distant planet, we know that God is present. We can commune with God who is from everlasting to everlasting. What a marvelous sense of presence that is. God provides a meal that will last through God's divine presence.

---

4   Buzz Aldrin, "Communion In Space," *The Guidepost Treasury of Hope* (New York: Guidepost Associates, Inc., 1976).

5. On Being Unworthy

1 Corinthians 11:17-34

When I was a young pastor in my first church which was a rural congregation in northern Virginia, one of our church members refused to accept communion one Sunday. In talking with him later about his refusal, he said to me: "I could not take communion because I had sinned. If I took communion, I would be damned forever." Then he quoted from the eleventh chapter of First Corinthians. When I served as a summer missionary as a college student, two fellow missionaries from Texas refused to take communion with the other missionaries or with the people we were serving. These young missionaries came from a church that prohibited taking communion with anyone other than those in their own church. They believed in closed communion. This man and these students either felt that they were unworthy or others were unworthy to participate with them in communion.

The Apostle Paul faced a problem of misconduct in the church at Corinth which had affected their practice of communion. Members in that congregation were acting unworthily toward others and it had created a real problem in the church. Paul found the behavior in the church at Corinth a knotty problem indeed. The church was filled with factions and quarrels. A group would gather for the Lord's Supper, which was often a whole meal, a kind of "love-feast." These wealthy church members would arrive early for the meal because they didn't have to work. Those who arrived early ate everything that was provided. When some of the other members arrived later, there was nothing for them to eat. The members who arrived early were often not only self-indulgent but intoxicated as well. Their "love-feasts" were not occasions for worship, but were means to gratify their own appetites and treat others with disdain. Their behavior profaned the sacred table. To these persons, Paul wrote: "If you think I am going to give you folks any words of praise for what you are doing, you are wrong. You are acting in a very unworthy manner at the Lord's table!"

The table of the Lord had been designed to be a door through which persons from all races and walks of life could gather together before the Lord. But their actions had closed that door and made it a wall — a barrier — that kept people out. The table of the Lord had been designed to be a window through which the light of God's love could shine upon all persons. But their actions boarded the window up, and the light of God's love and grace could not shine through. Today as we gather at the Lord's table, think with me a moment on these difficult verses from Paul's letter to the Corinthians about those persons who would eat the Lord's Supper in an unworthy manner, and thus be guilty of profaning the body. Those who "eat and drink without discerning the body, eat and drink judgment upon themselves," Paul writes. Or in some translations, it reads, "They eat and drink damnation upon themselves." Let me mention some insights I have found in my grappling with this difficult passage.

Look Within Yourself

I think Paul is instructing us first of all to look within ourselves before we eat the bread and drink the cup. Some translations read, "Test yourself." But Paul did not say what examination we are supposed to take before we eat the Lord's Supper. "Examine yourselves," Paul states, "to see whether or not you are eating in a worthy manner." Is Paul stating that we need to examine our lives as he instructed the Corinthians to examine their actions to see if they were betraying Christ and hurting his cause? Are we to ask ourselves the question that Judas asked Jesus at the Last Supper: "Lord, is it I?" The question, "Lord, is it I?" rings in our mind as we come to sit at the Lord's table. Have you and I not betrayed Christ at some time in our lives? You were faced with a difficult decision in your life. You knew the right thing to do, but rather than choosing what is right, you chose the wrong. You had opportunity to say a good word for Christ or his church, and you were silent. You had an opportunity to give something of your financial resources to help Christ and your church, but rather than do that, you used your money totally for pleasure. You had an opportunity to share the love of Christ with someone else, but you chose not to say anything. Are there not times that you and I, when we are honest, have betrayed our Lord? Examine yourself. Look inwardly and examine your own heart. Introspection for a moment will reveal that none of us is faultless. We are indeed sinners.

Selfish Motive

Reflect for a moment and examine your motive as you come to the Lord's table. Is your desire to participate at his table basically selfish? Is your thought directed primarily to what Christ has done for you? As you come to this table, you remember that Christ has redeemed you. You have salvation. You share in the joy of the table because of what you receive. Do you ever ask yourself:

"Because I have experienced such love, what can I do to serve Christ and share his love with others?" "Examine yourself," Paul says. Look at your motive for being at the table.

An Unworthy Manner

But, be careful. Many people wrestle with feelings of being unworthy already. The word in Greek which Paul uses here is an adverb. It refers to "an unworthy manner." He is not speaking about unworthy persons but about unworthy behavior. Too many persons live with feelings of unworthiness. They feel unworthy because they are too short, or too tall. They were born on the wrong side of the track, or their folks have too much money. They don't have enough education, or they have too much education. They are too poor or too rich. They wear glasses, or they can't hear well. Their skin is not the right color. Their hair is curly or their hair is straight. They are too young or too old. They have a physical weakness or a deformity. They have failed or committed some sin in the past. These feelings cause them to feel unacceptable and unworthy.

Acknowledge God's Acceptance

Many people have a feeling of being unworthy already. But that is not what Paul is talking about here. Remember to accept your acceptance by God. God does not reject us because of weakness or sin. Jesus ate with sinners. He said that he had come "not to call the righteous, but sinners to repentance." He came to seek and save sinners. When you and I come to the Lord's table, it is not that we have to make ourselves morally good. We do not have to make ourselves worthy to be acceptable to God. We come to the Lord's table and accept God's acceptance of us. We have already experienced his love for us in what he has done for us in Jesus Christ.

When Martin Luther was a young monk in the monastery, he wrestled with his own sins and feelings of unworthiness. He drove the priests crazy confessing one sin after another. In one confessional session, which was six hours long, he confessed every possible sin he could remember that he had committed. But as soon as he would leave the confessional booth, he would remember that he had forgotten some other sin! One of his Father confessors got so aggravated with him one day he said; "Look here, if you expect Christ to forgive you, come in with something to forgive — parricide, blasphemy, adultery — instead of all these peccadilloes."[5] But Luther found that his confessions did not bring him relief. He later discovered through his study of the Bible that "the just shall live by faith," and that "by grace are we saved through faith, not of works." We do not have to do something to deserve God's grace. We accept God's acceptance of us.

We come to the Lord's table aware that we are all sinners. We are ALL sinners, sinners saved by grace. Even as Christians, we are not free of sin. We come to the Lord's table and examine our attitude. We come remembering God's great sacrifice and gift of love for us, and we accept them. We begin by looking inward.

Look Around Yourself

Secondly, I think, Paul is telling us to look around us. Look at others who gather at the Lord's table with you in church. Paul reminds us that we have to "discern the Body of Christ" (v. 29). What kind of discernment are we to exercise? I think it is unfortunate that sometimes we

5   Roland Bainton, *Here I Stand: A Life of Martin Luther* (New York: Abingdon Press, 1950), 54.

come to the Lord's table and we do not realize the sacredness of this act. Paul Tillich wrote years ago in his book, *The Protestant Era* that "the sacraments have lost their spiritual power and are vanishing in the consciousness of most protestants."[6] Many of us have lost our sense of the sacredness of the Lord's Supper. Most Protestants are seldom aware of the fact that we are on holy ground during the observance of the Lord's Supper. When we have communion in our congregations, especially in Baptist churches, there seems to be a desire to rush through the service. Our mind wanders, and we do not focus on the meaning of the observance. We often want to get that part of the service over quickly so we can rush home, watch the ball games, eat our meal, or get to the restaurant before others do. The attitude seems to be: Don't make us late. We have another very important date. Don't make us tarry too long here.

God's Presence in the Present

Often we have no sense of the presence of God in the present. We have little awareness of the one who is here at the table, seeking to commune with us as the Bread of Life. Writing to the Corinthian church, Paul condemned the appalling manner which many took in observing the Lord's Supper. In not discerning the importance of the communion meal, Paul said that they were "eating and drinking judgment upon themselves" (1 Cor. 11: 29-31). They treated it as an ordinary meal and greedily ate most of the meal before others arrived, and they had little or nothing to eat. They were guilty of becoming spiritual sloths in not discerning the sacredness of the act of Holy Communion. The sacredness of the meal was made com-

---

6 Paul Tillich, *The Protestant Era* (Chicago: The University of Chicago Press, 1957), xix.

mon, and they profaned the holy and made it ordinary. The meal which should have led them to commune with the Bread of Life became an occasion for closing the avenue into the presence of the eternal one. Too often we gather at the Lord's table and do not discern the sacredness of the moment. Our behavior, like the Corinthians to whom Paul referred, makes a mockery of the sacred meal and dishonors our Lord.

Look Further to the Larger Christian Fellowship

But I believe there is also another problem which Paul alluded to in this passage. We often do not discern the importance of the unity of the body of Christ — his church. When you and I come together at the Lord's table, this is not a private affair. We come to commune with fellow Christians. The Corinthian church had shown careless disregard for others. Those who arrived early were concerned only with gratifying their own appetites and were unconcerned about their brothers and sisters who arrived late. Before you and I dismiss this and say that is not our problem today, let us be honest and admit that too often when we come to the Lord's table we are not really concerned about our brothers and sisters either. There is no sense of solidarity and bond with other church members.

The *Didache*, an ancient Christian writing, enjoined the Christians: "let none who has a quarrel with his fellow join in your meeting until they have reconciled, lest your sacrifice be defiled" (XIV: 2). First reconcile yourself with the person with whom you have a quarrel before you come to the Lord's table. Wasn't that similar to what Jesus said? "If you are offering your gift at the altar, and there remember that your brother has something against you, leave your gift there before the altar and go; first be reconciled to your brother, and then come offer your gift" (Matt. 5:23-24).

The Importance of Unity

I am convinced that divisions, divisiveness, and factions in the Body of Christ — the church — are heresy. It is nonsense to say that the church is strengthened by divisiveness. It always destroys the fellowship and hurts the church. Walter Rauschenbusch reminds us that "humanity always crowds the audience-room when God holds court."[7] Your redemption is always personal, but it is never private. As a Christian, we are also concerned about where our brothers and sisters are in their pilgrimage of faith. If we have a quarrel with another Christian, are upset with them, and it causes division in the Body of Christ, it hurts the cause of Christ.

The Table Sometimes Divides Us

One of the tragedies and heresies of the church is that the Lord's table, which should depict the unity of the church, is often the example of our worst dividedness. When I was a pastor in Kentucky, I served as the Chairman of the Commission on Christian Unity for the Kentucky Council of Churches. One fall our commission sponsored a conference at which we had a service of worship and communion. One of the most satisfying features of this worship service was to see persons from all denominations — Catholics, Lutherans, Episcopalians, Presbyterians, Methodists, and others — gather together to take communion at the Lord's table. But a sad fact was that there were some present that would not — could not — partake of the communion. It is a sad note that in the place where we should be the most united; often we are the most divided. It is sad, but more, I believe, it is heresy. The table that should unite us has too often divided us.

7   Walter Rauschenbusch, *A Theology for the Social Gospel* (New York: The Macmillan Co., 1917), 48.

The Unity in Christ

Paul instructed the Corinthians, "Let me tell you what you need to remember about this meal. I am passing on to you a tradition, not merely my words, but a tradition which goes back to our Lord himself. He took one loaf and one cup which symbolized the unity of his church — the togetherness of his people. He broke the bread and shared it with his disciples. And then the cup." Remember the unity of the church which the bread and cup represent. Remember the Christ who laid down his life that all persons might experience redemption. Remember that we are all brothers and sisters in Christ as we gather at his table. Remember he has commanded us to love one another. Let us work for unity of the church and seek to overcome our differences and quarrels with one another. Let us learn to love each other, even as Christ loved the church and gave himself for it.

All Are Forgiven by Christ

In a New Year's Eve worship service, the pastor of a church in Atlanta invited members of his congregation to come to the altar that night and confess silently any sins they had with a fellow church member. Two men, who had held a quarrel with each other for years, met at the altar rail that night. They stood before the altar looking at each other. They hesitated for a moment, and then they embraced and began to weep. Each asked the other to forgive him. They forgave past sins and began their lives as different men.

In a moment we shall come to the Lord's table. ALL of us have sinned. We come not because we are worthy, but because God loves us and we are saved by God's grace.

Unfortunately, too many of us have acted in an unworthy manner toward others. Let's ask for God to forgive us. Let's come to this table as a sign of our acceptance of God's acceptance of us and our acceptance of others as our brothers and sisters in Christ.

6. A Reminder in Your Hand

Psalm 103:1-2
Mark 14:22-24

Several years ago when my son and daughter were children, they gave me a key chain with a brass disk attached to it inscribed with the word "Dad" on it. I am sure that other fathers have something similar. I had it on my key ring for years and every time I used my keys, I had a reminder in my hand of my children because of this gift from them.

We all have "reminders" of various kinds in our pockets or purses. Some of you, for example, may have an Indian head penny that someone gave you years ago, and you keep it as a reminder of your friend or relative. Others of you may carry a silver dollar or a five or ten dollar gold piece. Some of you women have even had your five dollar gold piece mounted into a necklace. Some of you may carry with you a piece of colored glass, or a cross, or something else.

We all seem to want some kind of reminder to help us remember an important date or person, a wedding or an anniversary, a birthday or a graduation, or some other significant event in the past. We keep picture albums, calendars, date books, and scrapbooks to help us preserve our memories. Some of you make movies, video tapes, computer slides or cell phone pictures to keep your memories alive. You will return again and again to look at these.

Habits of Forgetfulness

Why do we go to so much trouble? Well, you know why. We are all such creatures of forgetfulness. If we do not have some tangible reminder, the past often becomes blurred in our memories. A story has made its rounds on university and seminary campuses about two professors who bumped into each other one day outside the administration building. One turned to the other and asked, "Would you like to go with me for lunch?" The professor scratched his head and thought for a moment and replied, "Now, when I met you, was I walking toward the library or coming from it?" "Why you were coming from it," the other professor responded. "Oh, then I have already had lunch."

Some of us have very short memories. We need somebody else to help us remember some things that may have happened even a short while before. When I was doing graduate study at Emory University, Charles Hartshorne, who was one of my professors, turned to the class on the last day of the seminar and asked the students: "Have all of you turned in your papers?" "Yes, sir!" we all said. "Then," he said, "All I have to do is find them." That is one of a student's biggest fears, isn't it? You spend all the time writing a paper, and then your professor loses it. Absent-minded professors are a part of every university and seminary campus. Absentmindedness or poor memories, however, are not limited to professors. All of us have to be prodded to remember better.

Our country has often used rallying cries to help people remember significant events. To encourage our soldiers on to victory, the cry went out, "Remember the Alamo," and "Remember the Maine." After the Japanese bombed Pearl Harbor, the alarm was sounded: "Remember Pearl Harbor." Remember! If we do not remember our past, then we are often destined to repeat the same mistakes.

Remembering Our Identity

We need to remember our roots and origin. We need to ask ourselves these questions: Who are we as a person? What is our identity as a nation?

What is the identity that makes us a person? A thief was caught after he broke into a house, and the caption in the paper read: "The man was identified as a thief, but his true identity is not known." Many of you have identification, but what is your true identity? Who are you as a real person? If you do not know your roots, origins, and the past out of which you have come, then sometimes you do not really know who you are. Memory is our collective consciousness. Our scrapbooks of memory enable us to understand more fully who we are. They tie us to the past, and the past enriches our present. These visible tokens and reminders of what we were and how we have lived enable us to know better who we are as persons today.

One of the finest gifts that First Baptist Church in Bristol, Virginia, gave us when we left after a nine-year ministry with them was three scrapbooks of letters from the congregation. These letters were written by adults, young people, and children. Various members of the congregation shared with us their feelings about what our ministry had meant to them over these years. Since leaving, on low days, I have often reached back into those scrapbooks of letters to find strength. Good memories from the past can often sustain us in difficult times in the present. We all occasionally need to draw on the storehouse of positive memories from the past where we have felt affirmation. This healthy memory will strengthen us in the present.

The Biblical Call to Remember

The Scriptures have many references about remembering. They remind us again and again to use our memory. The writer of the Book of Deuteronomy called the children of Israel to remember. "Remember," he said, "when you were slaves in Egypt and the Lord your God brought you out of that land of bondage into this free land flowing with milk and honey. Remember what God has done for you." He also told them to remember that God had promised that they would come to cities which they had not built, that they would drink from cisterns which they had not built themselves, that they would harvest grapes from vineyards which they had not planted. "Remember," he reminded them, "what God has done for you." Never, never forget it!

The Exodus was an event etched on their memory, and they were reminded again and again as a nation to remember what God had done for them. "Remember the sabbath day to keep it holy." "Remember that there is only one God, and He is the Lord God." "Remember the covenant which God has made with you," the prophets preached again and again to the nation of Israel. Remember it.

The psalmist cried: "Bless the Lord, O my soul, and forget not all his benefits." To put it in a positive way, he was calling them to remember everything that God had done for them. He summoned his whole being to praise. "Bless the Lord oh my soul." With this phrase, the psalmist was speaking to himself. He was addressing his whole being. To him, his soul was his heart, kidneys, bowels, stomach — the total being. Remember to bless God with your inner self, with everything that you are. We would translate that image today: "Use your mind, heart, strength, and feelings, spirit — your total personality — as you praise God." Draw on everything within you as a person to express thanksgiving to God for what God has done for you.

In autobiographical reflection, this writer draws upon his memory of God to assist him in times of need. In his moments of distress God came to his assistance. Memories from his personal experience fill his mind, and he is jubilant in his praise. He remembers the unchanging love of God and reminds himself that God is the source of all things. The verbs alone indicate how this writer has felt the impact of God in his life. He has affirmed that God has forgiven him, redeemed him, healed him, crowned him, sanctified him, and that God works for him in the world. His mind is filled with the goodness of God.

Remember what God has done for you in your own life. Remember that life itself comes as a gift from God. Remember that all you have — the air you breathe, the water you drink, the soil that gives you food, and the universe in which we live — all come as God's gift. Remember... Remember... REMEMBER! "Count your blessings," the psalmist reminds himself. "Name them one by one. Remember what God has done for you." As you step into the new year, remember the God who goes before you.

When we turn to the New Testament, we discover in the Apostle Paul's letter to the Corinthian church, which may have been the earliest written tradition about the Lord's Supper, his words of instruction. "Do this in remembrance of me." This meal is a memorial. "For as often as you eat the bread and drink the cup, you proclaim the Lord's death." Remember when you celebrate this event what it stands for. Most New Testament scholars are convinced that when Jesus took the Last Supper with his disciples, it was most likely the Passover meal that was observed. In observing the Passover meal, the youngest child would ask this question at the appropriate time, "Why is this night different from all other nights?" Then the father would explain to the child that this meal symbolized God's deliverance of his people from captivity. "Remember," the meal and words said. When we gather to observe the Lord's Supper, it is a call to commemoration. Remember. Focus your memory on what God has done.

The Eucharist's Symbols for Remembering

Have you ever asked yourself, "Why did Jesus select bread and wine as symbols for remembering? Why didn't Jesus take a coin as he had before and say, "Remember that you cannot build your life on material things"? Why did he not take salt and say, "You are to be the salt of the world; you are to be the element that gives it savor"? Why did he not take a piece of leaven and say, "You must be the penetrating force for good in society"? Why didn't he take water and declare, "I am the water of life"? Why did he not take a towel and basin and say, "I have washed your feet to give you an example; I have called you not to be ministered unto but to minister to others"? Why did he not take a whip and say, "I have told you that my Father's house is not a den of thieves but a house of prayer"? Why did he not take a fishnet and say," I have called you to be 'fishers' of men"? Why did he not take a stone and say, "This stone symbolizes the one that was rolled away from the tomb of Lazarus; remember I am the resurrection and the life"? Why did he not take the Scriptures and say, "You search the Scriptures because you think life is found in them, but it is they that testify of me"?

All of these things he had already told them. And they are all true. But when it came time to leave some lasting memorial with them, he took bread and a cup so that they would have a concrete memory of his suffering and death. The broken bread and cup symbolized his body and blood for them. He wanted them to have a familiar image to help them remember his suffering and death. The Gospel writers gave more space to the passion narratives than all the rest of the life of Jesus. They knew his suffering and death were central. He wanted them to remember his suffering and death when they observed this Last Supper again. The Last Supper calls us to remember how Jesus agonized in the Garden of Gethsemane, the kiss of betrayal by Judas, his arrest by the chief priest's soldiers, the mock trial, Peter's denial, and how the disciples deserted him, the brutal beating from the whip, the rejection by the people as they choose another over him, and finally the thuds of the hammer blows as the nails were driven into his hands and feet and his cross was erected on that forsaken hillside.

Remembering Jesus' Sacrificial Death

Remember that Christ suffered and died for us. Remember his death because his death is the avenue that leads us to understand God's mercy and grace. The bread and cup remind us, as we partake of them today, that salvation is God's gift. We are all sinners, and none of us merits redemption; none of us has earned it. We ourselves are recipients of God's love. We received it. "God so loved the world that he gave his only son." Redemption is through his grace. Remember today as we gather at the table that salvation comes to us as God's gift. In Mark's Gospel it is God who is blessed, not the bread or wine. We express our prayer of thanksgiving to God for that love.

One day, as I was driving to one of the hospitals in Louisville, Kentucky, I passed a sign along the roadside which stated: "Drive Through–Attitude Adjustment!" I thought that must really be a fascinating place, if you can get your attitude adjusted just by driving through it. I looked up to see what store was advertising such a possibility. It was a liquor store. Yes! They can alter your attitude. There is no question about that. They can alter it. But their alteration is not for the better, is it? If our attitude is to be adjusted, as it really needs to be, it cannot be changed for the better through drugs or alcohol. A real attitude adjustment can come only through a new creation. It will come about as we experience the new birth, as we become God's children — his sons and daughters.

In just a few moments you will have in your hands the bread and the cup. These will come to you as a reminder of what God has done for you. Remember God's grace! Remember God's love! Remember that you and I are sinners saved by grace! It is God's gift to us. As you eat the bread and drink the cup, remember. The reminder is in your hand.

Let us go now to the Lord's table to sense God's presence. May we feel it strongly as we worship in Christ's name.

7. Learning To Eat At The Lord's Table

Exodus 16:14-21
Mark 14:22-25

You can tell a great deal about a person by the way he or she eats a meal. If a person gulps his or her food down in a rush without really tasting it, this indicates something about his or her attitude toward the food. Some people never eat a meal without watching television or reading a newspaper, book or a magazine. They almost ignore their food. Other people seem to delight in each bite. They savor their food and notice its color and texture. Eating is a pleasure for them, and it is a pleasure to prepare meals for these persons.

Our mood can also affect how we eat. If we are angry, depressed, grieving or lonely, it affects our appetite negatively. If we are happy, joyous, laughing and full of pleasure, our bodies are affected in a different way. When our life is pleasant and the company is good, a meal tastes better. Our moods affect our digestive system. Studies have indicated that our attitude at the time we eat a meal really does influence our physical well-being.

Our Attitude at the Lord's Table

If it is important how we eat physical food, think how significant our attitude is when we come to the Lord's table. The way we approach his table reveals something about our religious development. We often approach the Lord's table in haste, without any thought or preparation.

We sometimes remain detached during the service and often simply go through the motions of the service. It has become routine for us, without much meaning. And then, we wonder why we get so little from the observance.

In Milan, Italy, there is a house where a group of priests lived years ago. On the wall of what was once a dining room is a painting by Leonardo da Vinci, who was one of the most famous artists of all times. When you examine the painting on the wall, you can see a place in the lower middle section where someone cut a doorway. Why? Because the priests were unaware of the significance of Leonardo da Vinci's painting, and thought that it was much more important to be able to go directly into the kitchen from the dining room than to preserve this painting.

Many of us come to this table oblivious to the presence of the one with whom we are coming to commune. We are simply not aware of the sacredness of this occasion, and so we sit through it and miss the beauty, mystery, and wonder of the event. This morning I would like for us to think about ways of approaching the Lord's table that may enable us to commune more effectively.

Christ Is the Host of This Table

The first reminder that I would offer you today is this: Remember that Jesus Christ himself is the host of this Table. The Lord's table is not your table, nor my table. It is not this church's table. It is the Lord's table. Jesus Christ is the host. He is the one who took bread and broke it. He is the one who took the cup and shared it with his disciples. It was he who blessed the bread and the cup. It is he who is hosts us here at this table today. Jesus Christ is not simply *on* the table. He is *at* the table. He is *presence,* and he is *present* with us. Today we celebrate the one who is host because he was victor over sin and death. We come to this table at his invitation. He extends his hands to all Christians, all sinners who will trust him, to come and commune with him at His table. "Come unto me all ye who are weak and are heavy laden." "Wherever two or three are gathered together in my name, there I am in the midst of them." Remember Jesus Christ is the host at this table.

We Come to Receive

Secondly, remember that we come to this table to receive. It was Jesus himself who took bread and broke it and said that it represented his body. He took the cup and declared that it represented his blood. We are receivers — receivers of what he has given for us. As we come to this table, we acknowledge that we are sinners saved by grace. We are recipients of God's love, grace, and forgiveness. "For by grace are you saved through faith" — not by anything you do. Grace is God's gift. We receive it. "For God so loved the world that he *gave* his only begotten son." Grace is not something we earn but something we receive. We come to his table this day to be receivers — to receive his love, forgiveness, and redemption.

"This is my body," Jesus said. In Aramaic there is no verb for "is." Literally it reads, "This body." "This-body" is not concerned with past or present but with identification. The bread and cup are representatives of Jesus' sacrifice. It is almost humorous how some theologians have wrestled for ages over the verb "is" and its meaning in this particular phrase. Jesus probably never even used it. He was declaring that he is present with us as we receive him.

"This *(is)* my body for you," Jesus said. "For you, Peter. For you, James and Andrew. For all you twelve who are gathered here. It is for you that I lay down my life." But it is also for you and for me. Martin Luther said that authentic religion is always best expressed in personal pronouns. God didn't love us abstractly. In Jesus Christ we have seen God's love for us, and each of us is able to receive it now.

The Old Testament lesson today focuses on the manna which was given to the children of Israel in the wilderness. They were told that they could not hoard it. They had to gather it fresh each day. What a powerful lesson for all about our relationship to God. Many persons live with the naive notion that they can drop-in on God anytime they want. They think they can "feed" on God and then "store" up that experience without seeking a fresh experience. They worship God occasionally and then wonder why their religious life goes stale and flat. They do not understand why their religion seems worthless and doesn't sustain them during difficult times. Our experience with God must always be fresh. We have to come again and again to his table to be fed. We come again and again to worship, to confess our sins, renew our spirit and go forth to serve. Having received his forgiveness, love, and grace, his presence is made real in our lives, and then we can live more effectively for him.

We Gather to Express Thanksgiving

Thirdly, we gather at this table to express thanksgiving. Jesus took the bread and the cup. He took; he broke; he blessed; he gave; he said; and he blessed. He blessed and so must we. We bless God this day for what God has done for us through Jesus Christ. We gather at this table as a sign of our thanksgiving to God who cared enough for each of us that his son laid down his life that we might have life. One of the biblical words for the Lord's Supper is Eucharist. Eucharist means thanksgiving. We come to this table in thanksgiving for what God has done for us. As we take this bread and cup, it is a sign of our gratitude to God for what God has done for us through his love.

The New Covenant

But we also come to this table as a sign of covenant. Jesus said that this cup is the New Covenant. That night in the Upper Room was the end of the Old Covenant and the beginning of the New Covenant. The word "covenant" appears in the Scriptures from Genesis through Revelation. God made a covenant with Abraham, Moses at Mt. Sinai, and with other prophets. God established a covenant relationship with his people. But Israel broke the covenant again and again. They assumed that they had a special handle on God.

Jeremiah prophesied that the day would come when the covenant which had been written in stone would be written on the human heart. In that upper room where Jesus took bread and broke it and took a cup and shared it, that was the beginning of the new covenant. At that moment the covenant was written on the human heart as a new community emerged. You and I are a part of that covenant community when we commit our lives to Christ and pledge our loyalty to him. As the new community, we covenant with one another to bear each other's burdens, and support each other in times of need. We draw strength from each other and the Lord of the new covenant. Each time we eat at the Lord's table is a sign of the covenant. It is a sign of our covenant with Christ and his covenant with us, and our covenant with one another as his people. So, let us come to his table this morning and pause to reflect on how we eat this meal.

Several years ago, Andrew Wolfe, visited West Berlin. One night, as he was walking from his hotel, he passed a bombed-out cathedral. Nothing but the shell of the cathedral was left. As he approached the cathedral, he noticed a statue standing in front of the church. He could see that the figure was chipped and battered in many places, and one hand was missing. On drawing closer to the figure, he realized that it was a statue of Christ. The statue stood with his hands outstretched. At first, he thought this was a sacrilege and wondered why they didn't replace it with a new statue. But as he got closer to the statue, the eyes of the Christ figure seemed to telegraph a message. "It was for this, exactly this that I had to come; to bear in my own body the signs of a broken world, and a broken humanity." At that moment the words of Jesus at the institution of the Lord's Supper came to him: "This is my body which is broken for you." The words took on new meaning for him. "Before they had been simply words out of a ritual, but there in the bombed-out shell of a church in a city divided by hostility, I understood their real meaning. A broken body for a broken world; that's what they mean."[8]

A minister friend of mine Don Harbuck, who died too young, penned the following lines in 1970:

THE TABLE
Two worlds —
one to believe in
one to live in
and between

8 Andrew R. Wolfe, "Broken Bread for a Broken World," *Pulpit Digest* (September-October, 1984), 3-4.

no bridge but a dream
Root out of dry ground
heat-choked at midday
impatient, parched
in the long afternoon just begun.
memory-haunted
by bread and wine around the table of togetherness
where presence is real
body and blood and word
felt and touched and tasted.
yet always
at the end
a parting into night
with frail souls
clutching crust and cup
in fingers of hope.
stumblers in the dark
spoiled by light
condemned to search
endlessly
for love's table
where belief and life
embrace.

Christ was broken for the brokenness of humanity that we might be drawn back to God. We come to this table today aware that we are all, in so many ways, broken persons — sinners all — but through his broken body we find wholeness and redemption. Let us come to his table with faith and expectation.

8. A Time For Celebration

LUKE 15:11-32

In some Christian traditions, the observance of the Lord's Supper is often called a celebration. Some of these traditions speak about celebrating the Eucharist, celebrating communion, or celebrating the mass. I think celebration is a good term for this sacred observance. It is biblical, because we celebrate many New Testament emphases when we come to the Lord's table.

An Example from the Prodigal Son Parable

Let's look at the parable of the prodigal son and its focus on celebration this morning. A young man found himself lost in a far country, but came to himself, rose up and returned home to find an opportunity for forgiveness and a new beginning. For a few minutes, let's look at that familiar old parable that Jesus told which has been called the prodigal son or the loving father. We have heard this parable many times and we know it well. I want us to look at the latter part of this parable and see if we can pick up a few lessons from it. I want us to focus on three basic thoughts: redemption, reunion, and rejoicing.

Redemption

First, notice what this parable teaches in the latter part of its story about redemption. The parable depicts the father telling his older son why he was welcoming back his prodigal son. In expressing his joy in having his son home, the father says: "He was dead and is alive again." We are all too familiar with posters which depict the faces of children who have been kidnapped or disappeared for some reasons. We have seen their faces in newspapers, on milk cartons, billboards or other places. Parents make many desperate appeals to find their missing child. The story in our text for today tells about a father who thought that his son was dead, but he discovered that he was not dead but alive! Why did he think his son was dead?

Searching for himself. Well, for one thing, his son really did not know who he was, did he? He had run off trying to find himself. In an attempt to discover who he was, he asked his father for his part of the family's inheritance. If he got his one-third, he thought he could do his own thing. All of us struggle with this same kind of feeling from time to time. We express this attitude with phrases like: "Well, I really wasn't myself today." "I don't know what made me do that. I was out of my head." "1 was just a fool and let myself go." There are times when we do not know who this I/me/he/she creature really is. We struggle for our own identity. We want to have our way. — do our own thing.

A number of years ago at a veteran's convention, a former G. I. went to the platform and made an appeal. "Is there anyone here who can tell me who I am?" He had suffered from amnesia for years and did not know his identity. You may not have amnesia, but you still may not know who you are. But he also did not know where he was going. He went rushing off with all the possessions he had, but ever so quickly he had wasted them in riotous living. Soon he found himself in famine and want. You may have heard about the man who got off his plane which had circled for forty-five minutes before it finally landed. He and a friend rushed into a taxicab and exclaimed: "We are late. Take us quickly. Move! We have to get there. Drive as fast as you can!" So the taxi driver took off. He had been driving about four or five minutes and the man asked: "Are we there yet?" "You didn't tell me where to go," the cab driver said. "You just told me to drive, and I have been driving!"

That is a parable about how many of us live, isn't it? We are busy going, going, and going. But we don't know where we are going. We are racing in every direction we can as we try to do what everybody else is doing. We are busy chasing what we think gives meaning to life. But sooner or later we will find ourselves in a wilderness experiencing famine like the prodigal son.

Came to himself. Redemption became possible when the prodigal son "came to himself." Some scholars are convinced that Luke, the physician, was using a medical term when he said the lad "came to himself." It was an expression of one coming to after he had fainted. He had fainted from hunger, but when he came to himself, he was aware that something was not right in his life. Something was radically wrong. He had been asking: "Give me. Give me." Now he pleaded: "Make me." "Make me as one of your hired servants." His life was changed in the "far country." There he realized that he had come to a dead end street. At this point, he decided to return to his father and ask for forgiveness.

The New Testament is filled with images that depict new beginnings. It speaks of "passing from death to life." As a sinner, we find our new beginning. We experience our own spiritual resurrection. We are raised up from the deadness of our sins and begin a new way of life as redeemed persons. Redemption moves us from death to life, ruin to resurrection and from selfishness to salvation.

Reunion

This parable also describes the reunion which the prodigal experienced. "This is my son who was lost and is found." The son really didn't know where he had come from. He had been cut off from his roots. He had severed himself from his father, his brother, and his whole family by asking for his inheritance before his father's death. His request in the eastern tradition was literally saying to his father: "I wish you were dead so I could already have what is legally mine." He cut himself off from his family and sought his own desires. He ended up in want and in a desperate situation. When his father saw his son at a great distance, he went running toward him to welcome his son home again. The son had run away, now his father ran to greet him. Sometimes God does just wait and let us do our own thing until we end up down some dead-end street in a wilderness or in famine and come home to him. But the picture of God sitting back and waiting is not the only image we have of God in the parables of Jesus. In this same fifteenth chapter, God is depicted in the parable of the lost sheep like a shepherd who goes seeking his lost sheep. Sometimes God waits. But God is also the God who is constantly seeking to bring us back from our wandering.

A God who welcomes. Whether God finds us in the wilderness when he comes after us or whether he is waiting for us to return home, we will always experience his outstretched arms that welcome us back. He does not want us to remain separated and isolated from him. He welcomes us home. When his son came back, his father said, "Bring the best robe." This best robe would have been the father's own. Who else would have the best robe but the father? "Put a ring on his finger." This was likely a signet ring indicating authority. The father noticed that his son was barefooted. That was a symbol of a slave. "Put sandals on his feet," his father cried. He had already been kissing and tenderly embracing his son. "My son was lost and is now found." There was a great sense of joy in that reunion. God wants us to reach our arms out to others and welcome them no matter how "prodigal" he or she may have been, or what paths those individuals may have wandered down. As the father welcomed his prodigal son home, God wants us to welcome others at his table. As Christians, let us extend our hands and invite them to come to the Lord's table and experience his forgiving love with us. Let us say to sinners, "You are welcome."

Unfortunately, we don't always do that. I sometimes see even in church Christians who refuse to forgive others for some act that may have been done years ago. They don't speak to them today. Imagine Christians who don't speak to each other! That is so unlike the spirit of Christ. Think about it. I a sinner, who has been forgiven and welcomed back by God, does not speak to some other Christian because of some conflict in the past. Jesus reminds us that we should forgive as we have experienced forgiveness.

In the Second World War, Corrie Ten Boom and her family had been arrested by the Nazis and placed in concentration camps. She had seen her father, mother, and sister killed by the Nazis. After the war, she was able to forgive them and began to preach about forgiving others, even the Nazis with all the atrocities which they had done. One Sunday in Munich, a man walked up to her and extended his hand to her following a sermon she had preached on forgiveness. He told her that he too had experienced the forgiveness she talked about. She looked into his face and recognized him as one of the Nazi soldiers who had been in charge of her prison camp. Her hand was frozen and she could not extend it to him. She prayed for God to give her the grace to forgive this man as she had preached. After a few moments she said she felt the power of God flow through her and she extended her hand to this former Nazi soldier. You and I need to extend our hand to all persons and welcome them at the table of the Lord as he has welcomed us.

Rejoicing

Then finally notice that this parable teaches us about rejoicing. After the lost son had returned, the family began to be merry and celebrate. They had a feast. They killed the fatted calf. This meant that it wasn't going to be merely a family feast. The whole village would be invited. The fatted calf would have been too much for a family. They would have killed a lamb. The fatted calf meant that everybody was invited. This was to be a big celebration. The one person who missed out on the joy and festivity of this occasion was the elder brother. He, because of self-righteousness, selfishness, stubbornness, anger and self-pity, remained outside and refused to come in. This parable was originally directed at the Pharisees. The elder brother symbolizes religious persons — you and me and all the Pharisees of life — who remain outside of God's love because we think religion is primarily a duty or a chore. The elder brother practiced religion but it had not really penetrated his life. He could not forgive, welcome back, and accept his brother. Suppose the prodigal son had met his elder brother first.

Church is family. This parable is trying to teach us that church is family. Our relationship to God is in community and family. When we are cut off from our family, we are cut off from each other and God. In our church family we join in celebrations at baptisms and weddings and bear each other's burdens during illnesses, sorrows and bereavements. Our church is a community of love and support, comfort and encouragement. It is a wonderful feeling to be a part of a church family and to know the joy of serving together. Images of family abound in this parable — father, son, brother, and home. To know that you are a part of this family of God in this community, in this church should bring you a sense of real joy.

Theodore Maudlin wrote about an experience he and his wife had at the end of the Second World War. They were sitting on the porch of one of their neighbors whose husband had been overseas for three years in military service. She had gone in to make them some tea. As they were sitting waiting for her to return, they saw a young soldier stop in front of her house at the gate and look at the house for a long time. Then he walked through the gate, up the front steps, did not notice them, walked inside, dropped his duffle bag on the floor of the hallway, and stood there for a moment. Then he whistled softly a familiar tune. The rattling of dishes in the kitchen stopped abruptly. The young woman raced into the hall and ran over to the young man standing there. Their fingers touched, and they looked at each other for a long time. No word was spoken. But communication took place. Then the young soldier reached down into his duffle bag and pulled out a package and said, "Darlin', here's the candy I went out to get for you." She spoke with a calmness that matched his. Her eyes, filled with happiness, were circled with crystals of tears. "Thank you, dear," she said, "but I think you were a long time getting it." Then they were in each other's arms. Maudlin and his wife tiptoed off the porch, walked through the gate, and went home.[9]

There is a reunion for every prodigal son or daughter where we can rejoice in the arms of God. There is always a marvelous reunion and celebration when a sinner comes home again. That's the good news of the gospel. We can come home again and experience God's love and grace. No matter how far we have wandered, what wilderness we have been in, what famine we have experienced, God welcomes us back, loves us, and celebrates our return with joy. Never forget that. It is good news indeed for us all. We come now to the Lord's table to celebrate his presence with us. Let's rejoice in the love which these symbols of bread and wine depict. Come with joy in your heart and thanksgiving on your lips.

---

9   Cited in J. Wallace Hamilton, *Horns and Halos in Human Nature* (Westwood: Fleming H. Revell Co., 1954), 159.

9. The New Covenant

Luke 22:7-20

All of us, even from the time we were children, have made some kind of covenant or contract with someone, some person, or some establishment. Even when we were young, we would make covenants to be on time for ball games. We would make covenants in scouting or some other kind of club. When we got old enough to purchase something, we would make a covenant that we would pay for a certain item some day, sometimes in ninety days, the same as cash. When we purchase a car, it usually takes longer than 90 days to pay for it, so we enter into a kind of covenant that we will pay for it. Then, of course, when we purchased a home, we would usually enter into a lengthy covenant. Those of us who are married made a covenant with someone, pledging our love, loyalty and support to that individual. So covenants are not unknown to us even today.

Covenants in the Bible

The Bible speaks a great deal about covenants, compacts or contracts. A covenant is an agreement that individuals make one with another. The covenant is one of the great teachings of the Bible. References to this covenant appear 286 times in the Old Testament alone. The Bible speaks about a covenant which was made between God and humankind. God selected the nation Israel as God's bride. "You are my chosen betrothed", God said to Israel. God entered into a covenant with them. But the covenant required them to be faithful. God entered a covenant with Abraham (Gen. 17). And later we read about the covenant relationship that God made with Moses on Mt. Sinai (Ex. 20). Prophets like Hosea, Amos, Micah, Jeremiah and others refer to Israel's covenant relationship with God. They spoke boldly about the unfaithfulness of Israel to that covenant and how God continuously called them back into the love relationship.

The New Covenant

Jeremiah said that one day there would be a new covenant. This covenant would not be centered on human conditions but would be written within the heart. Since Israel was unable to keep the old covenant, God brings about the consummation of the contract or covenant. In our text today Jesus refers to a new testament or a new covenant. The Old Testament or the old covenant was based on righteous living but Jesus Christ has issued in a new testament, a new covenant. The old covenant was based on law. The new covenant is based on love. The old covenant was based on the requirement of keeping rules and a person's loyalty to God. The new covenant is based on the grace of God. No matter how hard human beings try, men and women cannot keep the strict laws of the old covenant as they seek to worship God. Jesus said, when he took the cup, "For this is my blood of the covenant which is poured out for many for the forgiveness of sins" (Matt. 26:28).

The Blood Image

Most of us today are not very comfortable with the biblical talk about blood. We would prefer some psychological references. We would prefer some other kind of language which does away with that old image. In the ancient world, contracts or covenants were usually ratified in at least three ways. A covenant would be reached sometimes by the parties eating salt together. Salt was a rare thing in the ancient world. Sometimes they would ratify the covenant by eating a meal together. At other times they would sacrifice animals and walk through the carcasses or smeared some of the blood on each other's hands or dipped their hands in the blood. This bloody act was the way of symbolizing that an agreement was sealed.

For those of us who are uncomfortable with the concept of blood, we have to understand that the scriptures are very clear about this matter. In the scriptures, blood symbolizes the outpouring of God's life for us. We see how this pictorial image has been picked up by great poets like Handel's *Worthy Is The Lamb* or the popular hymn "Are You Washed In The Blood of the Lamb?" These writers draw on the images from the book of Revelation where it states, the angel replied, "They have washed their robes in the blood of the Lamb and they become white" (Rev. 7: 14). The concept of the blood is to depict the sacrifice and the costly nature of God's love. The image is of God emptying his life for us that we might have life. The focus is on our assurance that we cannot wash away our sins, but the Lamb of God takes our sins away.

The Costly Nature of Redemption

When a person is gravely ill, sometimes they have to have a blood transfusion. The transfusion of blood from one individual to another helps restore life. The symbolism here is that, when we give ourselves to God, there is a transfusion symbolically of God's blood into us that washes us clean and makes us whole again. If we attempt to dismiss this concept of blood, we will do away with the costly nature of redemption and the symbolism which the scriptures used to depict God's grace. We all suffer from guilt from things we have done. But the scriptures tell us that Jesus paid it all, and we are washed clean by God's grace and God's sacrifice *in* Jesus Christ.

In the ancient Greek world there was a legend about Prometheus. He was the man who stole fire from the gods. He was severely punished by the gods because of his actions. The people, though, held Prometheus up as a great hero, although the gods punished him out of their anger. When Jesus Christ sacrificed His life, no one looked up at God and said, "Isn't God an awful, angry God?" When Jesus died on the cross, his disciples said, "This shows us the sacrificial nature of God. This shows us how loving God is and how much God cares for us. And more, they pointed to the cross and said "God was in Christ reconciling the world to himself." God, somehow, was uniquely involved in that sacrifice. God was not remote. God laid down God's own life for you and me. This covenant has been ratified through the blood of Jesus Christ. He gave his life that we might have life.

A Commemoration

Notice also that Jesus declares that this meal is a commemoration. As we gather at the Lord's table, we are to remember to commemorate what Jesus has done. The cup and the bread both symbolize the blood which was shed and the body which was broken. They depict the life which was given so we might remember God's great love. What we will do in a few moments as we observe this memorial and what Jesus did was an "acted parable." It was a visible image, a dramatic representation of

His death. Through this dramatic act, Jesus was trying to plant *in* the memory of these men what His death was going to mean. In this presentation we have one of the rare sayings from Jesus about His own death. The Lord's Supper was a means of reinforcing the disciples' memory of the importance of the death of Jesus. After the resurrection, they would recall what Jesus had said at the Last Supper. And they would remember what *his* death really meant. The bread which was broken was to remind the disciples of the broken body of Christ. The wine which they drank was to remind them of the blood which Jesus shed for them. Both of these elements were tangible evidences of the work of Christ. In their memory of this event, the Last Supper would give them an experience that would enable them to translate and understand the rich meaning of his death.

The Redemptive Work of God

After the resurrection and *in* light of Jesus' death on the cross, the bread and wine would say to Jesus' disciples, "Remember me and my death." The words of our text, "This is my blood of the covenant, which *is* shed for many for the remission of sin" affirm the great redemptive work of God through Christ. The apostle Peter writes in one place, "Repent and turn that your sins may be blotted out," (Acts 3:19). The phrase "blotted out" is rich with symbolic meaning. For those of us who are older, we can remember writing with a fountain pen and having to use a blotter to make sure that the ink did not smear. The image here is more than just blotting ink. In ancient biblical times they would often write on a waxed tablet and sometimes a covenant would be sealed with a waxed inscription. A sharp pointed instrument would be used to write on the waxed tablet. If they wanted to erase it, they would take the blunt or flat end of the stylus and rub it over the waxed tablet. They could remove every mark that had been made there. This is the image that is used when it says, "God has blotted out" our sins. God has absolutely forgiven us and there is no trace of our sins. As the psalmist says, God has removed our sins "as far as the east is from the west." This is the wonder and mystery of God's redemption.

A Time of Remembrance

The Lord's Supper reminds us of what Christ has done for us through his death, and we gather at his Table to remember that sacrifice. The acted parable and the words which Christ used at the Lord's Supper are clear evidence of the estimate that Jesus placed on his own death. Christ's death was more than a revelation, more than an example, more than a martyr's death and more than a sacrificial death for a friend. It was a sacrifice for the sins of the world. From the beginning of Christianity, the church indicated that the death of Christ was at the center of its teachings. The cross is the central act of God's grace. Those who would remove the atoning death from the teachings of the Church have great difficulty in trying to explain the command from Jesus at the Lord's Supper which reads, "Do this in remembrance of me." His broken, sacrificial body has been the ornament that has filled the universe with the fragrance of God's redemptive grace. The celebration at the Lord's table is a continuous proclamation of what Christ has done for us. It is a memorial of him to proclaim the Lord's death until He comes again.

The Comprehensive Reach of God's Love

The new covenant of which Jesus speaks is also comprehensive. Jesus says, "This cup is the new covenant in my blood, which is shed for many." The cup dramatizes the outpouring of the blood of Jesus Christ to cleanse us of our sins. It affirms that God's grace is open to all persons. No one is excluded. Persons of all races, men, women, and children can all come and receive God's forgiving grace.

The new covenant reminds us that God's redemption is for all persons. No one is excluded. We can come and stand at the foot of the cross knowing that God's love extends to everyone. John tells us that, "God so loved the world that he gave his only begotten son that whosoever believes should not perish but have everlasting life," (John 3:16). Anyone who believes can receive God's redeeming grace.

A Call to Commitment

Finally, the new covenant speaks to us about commitment. When we come to the Lord's table to receive the bread and the cup, it requires of us commitment. We commit ourselves to receive these elements and in receiving them, commit ourselves to the Lord whom they represent. The broken bread and the cup symbolize the brokenness of Christ for us and the blood which was shed. They challenge us to commit ourselves to the Christ whose memorial we are depicting.

In some Christian traditions they have what is called a "eucharistic" offering. This offering underscores the commitment which the Christian makes at the time of communion. Think with me about the original meaning of the word "offertory." In the early centuries of the

Christian church, when Christians came to celebrate the Lord's Supper, they actually brought their offering of bread and wine and laid it on the altar to be used in the service of the Lord's Supper. That was the "offertory." In some parts of the eastern church it is still done today. That practice had to underscore in the minds of the early Christians their part in committing themselves to God.

Communion is a reminder to us that we offer ourselves to God. We commit all that we are to God - our work, our recreation - our financial support - our possessions - our total being to God. We consecrate all that we have and are to God. It is foremost an offering of ourselves. William Barclay, the noted New Testament scholar, describes an experience that took place on a train in Victoria Station in London a few years after World War II. Dr. Barclay says he was returning to Glasgow when two young men boarded the train and were seated in the compartment he was occupying. After the train had pulled out of the station, one of the men had an apparent epileptic seizure. He fell to the floor with violent convulsions. He began to writhe and tremble. His young friend picked him up and put him back on the seat and wiped the beads of perspiration from his face. He placed a pillow behind his head and covered him with a blanket.

After the man who had had the seizure, calmed down a bit, his friend turned to Dr. Barclay and said, "I am sorry. I had hoped this would not happen. He has these seizures about twice a month, and he just had one a few days ago. We did not expect one so soon." "You need not apologize," Dr. Barclay replied. "I understand, no problem!" "You can't really understand," the man responded. "My friend and I were in the Normandy invasion together. He is English, and I am an American. We were both wounded. My leg was blown off. My friend had shrapnel wounds all across his chest. A hand grenade had blown away much of his chest and shoulder. I don't know how he did it, but he got to his feet and dragged me to safety. I heard him crying with agony each step of the way."

The young American had become very emotional. He continued, "I kept telling him to go on and save himself, but he told me, 'No Way ... if you die. I die with you' and finally he got us to a medic station." "Two years ago," he continued, "I found out that he had this condition. I am single, so I sold my house and furniture, quit my job, cashed in my savings, and came over here to take care of him because he needs around the clock attention. It's all right now, because I am with him and I can serve him as long as he needs me." "Friend," Dr. Barclay said, "You don't have to explain anymore. That is the most beautiful and noble story I have heard in my life." "Man," the young man responded, "you still don't understand ... after what he did for me, there isn't anything I would not do for him."

That is the challenge we have from Jesus Christ. He gave his life for us. He sacrificed his all - his broken body, his blood - that we might have life. In the light of what he has done for us, it requires commitment from you and me. As we approach this table, let us not forget that great challenge. We come now to the Lord's table. Let us come confessing our sins. As we partake of the bread and the cup, let us remember that Jesus is present with us in the new covenant relationship. Let us celebrate his risen presence with us.

10. Communion In A Time Of Survival

Isaiah 1:11-18
John 6:41-60, 15:12-17

The saying from Jesus that his disciples must eat his flesh and drink his blood is not an easy one to accept. It is offensive to us and it was offensive to the people who heard it in Jesus' day. This saying was so offensive that many of them turned away and quit following Jesus. The New English Bible translates this phrase, "This is more than we can stomach! Why listen to such talk?" (John 6: 60). It was a hard word, and many could not accept it and would not and did not understand it. Many of us find the words which we have from Jesus that we must "eat his flesh and drink his blood" as probably among the hardest of his teachings.

I believe that Jesus was affirming that he came to give his followers something greater than the bread Moses gave the children of Israel in the wilderness. Moses was merely the means God used to lead the people to the bread he provided for them. Jesus is saying, "I am the bread." He was attesting that persons would find the relationship they wanted with the Father, through him. "I am more than just a means to it. I am the way." When you and I attempt to look at that saying and try to understand how it relates to us and our understanding of the Christian faith, it is still not easy. This is especially true when we try to relate it to our own everyday life. We often wonder how we can go about surviving and just living day by day. These words from Jesus seem difficult to fit into our lifestyle.

The Story of the Andes Survivors

Several years ago, I stayed up most of the night reading a true story written by Piers Paul Read entitled *Alive: The Story of the Andes Survivors*. A plane carrying forty-five people, most of whom had been in a rugby match in Santiago, crashed into the mountains in the Andes. Of the forty-five people on the plane, twenty-seven were still alive following the plane crash. When the plane fell into the freezing snow, it broke in half. The people had little clothing, and what they had was very light since they had been in a warm climate before. Among those who survived was a young man who had a steel rod sticking through his stomach. Others had broken bones and internal injuries. Only sixteen survived. They survived basically by caring for each other. Those, like the young man with the steel rod stuck in his body, assisted others who were hurt worse than they were. Those who were strong attempted to help the weaker ones. They had almost no food except for a few dates, some crackers, a little jelly, a few candy bars, and a bit of wine. They rationed the food to each other by breaking the crackers, the candy bars, and other items into tiny bites. They had no utensils, so they drank the wine from a deodorant can top. In a few days the food was all gone. But they survived for seventy-one days.

One of the young men there wrote these words: "It was something that no one could have imagined. I used to go to mass every Sunday, and Holy Communion had become something automatic." (All of the crash victims were Catholic.) "But up there, seeing so many miracles, being so near God, almost touching him, I learned otherwise. Now I pray to God to give me strength and stop me from slipping back to what I used to be. I have learned that life is love, and that love is giving to your neighbor.... There is nothing better than giving to a fellow human being."[10] Remember, they had such a small amount to give. Yet in that crisis situation, they learned a powerful lesson about life — the ultimate meaning in life is found in loving your fellow human being.

Not the Entire Story

But that is not all of the story. They were able to survive seventy days because they did find a food source. They had asked, "Where shall we get food?" As they were outside the plane disposing of some of the bodies of those who had died by placing them in the freezing snow, one of them said to another, "I know that if my dead body could help you to stay alive, then I'd certainly want you to use it."[11] They made a pact then that if others died, they would use their bodies for food. Finally after several weeks when all the food was gone and they realized that help was not going to come, they knew that there was only one way they could survive. They had to have nourishment.

One of them went outside and cut off some flesh from one of the bodies, put it on one of the plane wings to dry enough to eat. He then swallowed it and reflected: "It's like Holy Communion. When Christ died he gave his body to us so that we could have spiritual life. My friend has given us his body so that we can have physical life."[12]

10 Piers Paul Read, *Alive: The Story of the Andes Survivors*. (New York: Avon, 1974), 279-280.
11 *Ibid*, 77
12 *Ibid*, 83

They survived because they literally fed off those who had already given their lives. Several of them finally got strong enough from eating this meat that they were able to climb over the mountain and reach help for the others. In their first interview after they were rescued, they shared this with people, and many were shocked, and some were astounded. But the local priest did not condemn them and neither did most of the newspapers. For them, the act which they had participated in had become a spiritual experience.

The Mystery at the Lord's Table

Now what is Jesus telling us? Is it something like we have just described? Are we literally to feed off his physical body and be nourished? Is that what he is seeking to say? No. It is much more than that, I think. One of the things that he is saying here is that spiritual fellowship with him is one of the deepest mysteries in life. As we gather at the table of communion, we acknowledge boldly, openly, and emphatically that words are never sufficient to declare the costly grace and love of God. Our words always fail; they are inadequate and insufficient. We cannot express all of our faith. How can one wrap words around the mystery of God's love, and say, "I have explained it?" Do not listen to that person. The love of God goes beyond all human explanations. We can only hint at the greatness of God. We have sensed only the edge of God's garment.

I am convinced, after years in the ministry, that most people who do not commit their lives to Christ do not do it because there is some intellectual argument which has not been fully satisfied. For most people, it is a lack of personal commitment. It is an unwillingness to commit one's life to Christ, an unwillingness to step forward and commit one's life to him and acknowledge that part of our life is beyond one's total understanding. There is always the element of deep mystery involved in our understanding of God.

A Deep Inner Significance

What then do we make of these words of Jesus to help us understand the mystery? You and I must remember that in the day in which Jesus spoke the people were surrounded with all kinds of religion. They had what was called the mystery religions. Some of the ancient religions of nations around Israel would often prepare meat and offer it as a sacrifice to their god. They did not destroy all of the meat in their sacrifice. The people themselves would eat part of the meat which was prepared and offered to their god. They believed that when they ate some of the meat which was prepared for this god they literally took this god's presence into their body. By eating the meat, they were sharing in something of the vitality of the life of this god. Later Paul wrote to Christians in the Corinthian church who were very concerned about this very issue. (1 Corinthians 8: 1-13). They were asking whether or not they should eat the meat offered to idols? To them, this would be in some way acknowledging that they were taking this false god in to their being. You and I can call this attitude whatever we want to — superstition or nonsense. But they literally believed it. Jesus drew on the ancient beliefs which these people understood. But he was not telling them that they were literally to take his flesh and that would make them religiously vital. He was seeking to probe beneath the surface to tell them, and now us, that his presence in our lives has deep inner significance.

Penetrating Words

Raymond Brown in his *Commentary on John* tells us that these words probably go back to the primitive preaching tradition and that John has brought them forward here to tell us some truth about the Lord's Supper itself.[13] When we gather at the communion table, there is here a deeper significance than you and I can ever acknowledge about the presence of Christ in our lives. I have many books on my shelves. One of them is written by Jürgen Moltmann and entitled, *The Crucified God*. In this book, this German theologian describes what he believes the sacrifice of Christ means. But I can never learn anything from that theologian about the death of Christ if I never read his book and simply leave it on the shelf. To learn from it, I must read it and let it penetrate my mind and thought and become a part of me. No one can ever learn anything from the *Gospel of John* if he or she never reads it or never hears anybody discuss it. We must pick it up and read it and let it penetrate our mind and heart. At home I have a recording of Handel's *Messiah*. As long as it stays on the shelf, I cannot enjoy that music. But when I play it, it can come into my life and become a part of me. It penetrates me and I am uplifted by the power of that great music. So Jesus is telling us, "Unless I come into your life and penetrate it, unless you take me into your life and I become a part of you, then I am really not yours and I do not influence you."

Words from Isaiah

This is a part of what Isaiah was saying to Israel. The people had gathered in the temple. They offered all kinds of sacrifices to God. This included animal and cereal offerings. They also had special holidays which were

[13] Raymond E. Brown, *The Gospel According to John*. (Garden City: Doubleday & Co., 1966), 287.

designated as sacred and holy, but Isaiah said that all of this was utter foolishness because their religion did not touch their everyday life. Their religion had not changed how they treated their neighbor, how they treated their friends, the widow, and the needy. If religion is real, Isaiah is reminding us, it is more than just on the surface. It penetrates one's whole being. He was telling them and us that gifts are not enough. It takes generous living. Sacrifices are no substitute for service. Ritualistic religion is never a substitute for righteous living. Christ must penetrate our lives. As we partake of the bread and the cup, it is a symbolic way affirming the living presence of Christ as living Lord in our lives as we go into the world.

The Element of Love

Hear another word. When Christ comes into our lives, we are different because he introduces a new element into our being. That element is love. This element of love which comes into our lives penetrates us and gives us more than just an instinct for survival. Too often life is depicted as merely surviving. Lucy is standing by the door as Charlie Brown is going to school. She says, "You had better rush. You are going to be late. Here is your lunch." As he walks down the steps to leave, she says: "Survive!" For some of us, that is about all that we do in the world — survive. But Jesus said that he had come that we might have life. He is the living bread and when we learn to feast on him, he introduces into our life an element of love which is transforming.

A woman had come to a communion service. She was a noted prostitute and felt unworthy of taking the elements. A deacon in the church leaned over to her and said, "Take it." She hesitated. "It is for sinners," the deacon continued, "which we all are." The word which we receive from God is he has first loved us. He has loved us while we were sinners and has drawn us to himself. We come to his communion table to feed upon him and to experience the transforming love that he has given us. He has first loved us.

Jesus said, "This is my commandment that you love one another." "But wait a minute now, Jesus," we want to ask, "How can anybody command love? You can't just say, now children I want you to stand up here and love your parents. I want you to do this. I command it." Do you teach somebody to play the piano by saying, "I command you to sit down and play the piano? If you don't, I'm going to take a hymnbook and beat you across the head until you learn how to play it." No. You love them into learning how to play by giving them instructions, guidance, care, patience, and understanding. Christ comes into our lives and gives us through his patience, his care, his understanding, his grace, and the ability to learn how to love more lovingly as we are taught by him.

The Power to Love

The love that is introduced into our lives also gives us the means of loving as we care for other people. It is not always easy to love those who sometimes are unlovable. But that is a part of what Jesus is telling us to do. A minister, who was close to retirement, went one day to visit a woman who was a little older than he. She had been a school teacher for many years and had enriched the lives of people through her teaching. At one time she had been in love with a young man, and they had wanted to get married but for some reason they had decided not to and she had never married. She was sitting in a wheelchair during the visit, and after he finished his conversation with her and got ready to leave, he leaned over and kissed her on the forehead. She looked up at him and said, "Thank you. Not many people kiss me anymore."

There are a lot of people in the world that nobody ever kisses anymore. You and I need to be the means of sharing this love. We are a part of the means of going into the world where there are lonely, needy, hurting people and sharing with them the love of God through our lives. We say to them, "I love you in the name of God."

Loving Directions

The love that Jesus Christ gives our lives gives us direction in how to live and care. He tells us that authentic life, when we feed on him, is the loving life. It is not just a life of survival, but it is a loving way, a way filled with meaning and richness because we are daily feasting upon him. Jesus said, "I call you no longer slaves but friends… and I lay my life down for you." If Jesus Christ has laid his life down for us, we in turn are called and challenged to lay our lives down in service and ministry for him.

During the Second World War at the German concentration camp in Ravensbruck, a Russian Orthodox nun was a prisoner there. She was deeply loved by all, even the German soldiers. She had been a prisoner there for two and a half years and they probably never intended to put her to death because she did so much good in the camp. At one of the daily gassings, a young woman in line to be gassed was so frightened that she broke down and began to cry. Mother Maria slipped over and pushed her aside and said, "Don't be frightened. Look, I will take your turn." She went into the gas chamber unnoticed, and later when they discovered that they had gassed her by mistake, it was noted that the gassing stopped for several days.[14] She didn't bring an end to the horror. But,

14 Victor Gollancz, *A Year of Grace*. (Gollancz, 1950), 209.

because of her sacrificial love and death, she brought an end to it for a while.

God has never promised us that if we stand up and live or die for him, that we will put an end to all evil, pain, and suffering in the world. But your life and my life, as we love, can help to make a difference for a little while. If there are enough of us who are Christ-like in our loving, think of the impact it will make in the world.

Father, as we commune at the Lord's table, feed us with your presence. May your sacrificial love penetrate our lives so we can live more like our Lord. Amen.

11. A Christmas Eve Communion Meditation:

"Are You in the Mood for Christmas?"

Judges 13:8
Matthew 2:1-3

On this Christmas Eve, we are preparing to come to worship at the Lord's table. Are you ready to celebrate Christ's presence with us this sacred night as we eat the bread and drink the cup? Can you affirm anew your belief in the incarnation that came in the form of a baby in Bethlehem two thousand years ago? Are you in the mood to attest to his sacrificial death which we acknowledge at this sacred table tonight? What's your mood on this Christmas Eve? Are you really in the mood for the deep meaning of Christmas? Many of us have trouble getting in the mood for Christmas or discovering "the Christmas spirit." Some, it would appear, may never get in the mood.

The Annunciation

Many are surprised to learn that the annunciation to Mary about the birth of Jesus was not the only annunciation in the Bible. A number are found within the scriptures. In the book of Judges, an angel appeared to Hagar and announced the promise of the birth of a child who would be named Samson. But, like Joseph in the New Testament story, Manoah, Hagar's husband, had difficulty believing his wife's story. He asked for a return visit of the messenger to get the story from him. Manoah asked the messenger a question which has resounded through the centuries, not just for this child, but especially for the child called Jesus. "What shall we do with this child?" This question is not merely the curious inquiry of Manoah and Hagar for their child, but the question of all parents as they face the upbringing of their own children. But more importantly in this Christmas season it is the question which each of us must ask about the birth of Jesus, the one who was born centuries ago. What will you and I do with this child?

Cynicism

Our response to this child is reflected in various ways and through different moods. Some approach Christmas in a mood of cynicism. Scrooge-like they declare that Christmas is just for children. We are so familiar with Christmas and all its traditions that it no longer has real meaning for us as adults. Our children are grown. And we have lost our sense of excitement, anticipation, hope, joy, and wonder. Yes, Christmas is for children but also for those who are still child-like in our faith — trusting and young at heart. Phillips Brooks reminds us in one of his hymns, "The earth has grown old with its burden of care. But at Christmas it is always young." Remember that Jesus taught us that only those who were child-like would enter his kingdom.

Secularism

Others find themselves caught up in the mood of secularism at Christmastime. Many say that Christmas has become so secularized that its real meaning is slowly disappearing. Now, this is always a danger. There is no question that this could happen. In the seventeenth century, when the Puritans were in political power, they made the observance of Christmas illegal. Fancy pies and plum puddings were banned and even worship wasn't allowed on December the 25th. They tried to remove all aspects of Christmas from the lives of the people.

I don't know about you, but I would hate to live so far removed from civilization that I could not participate in any of what is often designated as the commercialization of Christmas. I enjoy the lights. I enjoy walking or driving down streets where stores and houses are decorated. I like the hustle and bustle which comes from shopping in the season. Even when my shopping is done, I like to walk through the mall and watch people as they rush to finish their shopping. I sense a spirit in the air. Something would be missing in my Christmas if I were on some desert island and couldn't see and hear the many sounds of Christmas, even the commercialized ones. A friend told me that her son and wife lived in a foreign country where no mention was made about Christmas. "They longed," the mother said, "for even a commercial on television about Christmas."

Christmas, of course, can become distorted by commercialization. But I am convinced that some of the people who get caught up in the commercialism of Christmas are caught up in it all the time anyway. If you are a sucker for buying things at Christmas, you are probably a sucker at other times as well. If you can be pushed into spending too much at Christmas, you likely spend too much on other occasions too. Store merchants and commercial salespersons cannot determine what the real meaning of Christmas is for others. I think it is great that we have a nation that puts such glitter and glamour on this event and toots a loud horn for the celebration of the birth of

Christ, even if it is slightly distorted. All of this celebration makes us aware that something unusual and unique is going on here.

Several years ago, when we were looking for our Christmas cards, Emily, my wife, picked a card off the rack, held it up, and asked: "What do you think of this one?" I knew that this was not the one we would send by the tone of her voice. She read the greeting inside. "Christmas is a wonderful way to round out the year." Now, if that is your card, I am sorry. But somehow or another it doesn't convey to me the authentic meaning of Christmas. "Christmas is a good way to round out the year." What are they talking about? Christmas is more than that in the mind of a Christian. Yes, there is always some danger of Christmas becoming secular. But we must always remember that Christmas focuses on the fact that the Word became flesh. God came into a secular world so that we could more clearly sense the reality of God's presence.

Impatience

Some have difficulty waiting patiently for Christmas to arrive. They approach Christmas with a mood of impatience. They are like John the Baptist and other Jews who were looking for the coming of the Messiah. They wondered if Jesus were really the Messiah. From his prison cell, John the Baptist asked Jesus the question: "Are you the one we are looking for?" He impatiently wanted to know whether God had answered the prayers of his people for the coming of the Messiah.

Some of us are still impatient with God's ways. We would never have chosen the way God selected to come into the world and tell people about God's love for humanity. We would not have come in the form of a baby. We would likely have come with marching armies, with a king or some political leader who had great power and prestige. But God picked the backside of nowhere and a humble, peasant woman to be the divine instrument. People had waited centuries for God to come, and they were often very impatient. But so are we.

Impatience is something we all have to live with, especially at Christmastime. Children can hardly wait until Christmas gets here. On Christmas Eve, many cannot fall asleep until late as they wait with anticipation for what Christmas morn will bring. If you don't think people are impatient, stall your car at a traffic light. We are living in an age where people want their needs met immediately. We are in the age of the instant steaks, instant tea, and instant coffee, instant replays on TV, iPhones, cell cameras, and microwave ovens. We want our food and everything else ready instantly. But God doesn't always work that way, does he? God took centuries to prepare a nation before he sent his son as Savior. You and I may want results in a moment. But God patiently works his way in the hearts, and lives of people ever so slowly. God is a God who can wait. He is not in a hurry. But ... so often we are.

Busyness and Rushing

This leads me to the mood which often characterizes Christmas — rushing. We read that, when the announcement was made to the shepherds at the birth of the Jesus in Bethlehem, they all came "with haste" to see the baby. At its point of beginning, Christmas seemed to put everything in motion. Not only were the shepherds put in motion at the first Christmas but so were the wise men and Herod.

Centuries later, Christmas still seems to put everything in motion. Everyone is in a rush with baking, buying gifts, decorating, and traveling to see one's family. Nobody seems to have enough time for anything. This was illustrated for me in a Ziggy cartoon. "I never manage to get my Christmas cards mailed on time," Ziggy said, "but this is the earliest I have ever been late!" We can identify with that, can't we? We don't seem to have time for all that needs to be done. We are pulled in so many directions. We are so busy with our rushing to get all of our work done that we can't celebrate Christmas.

A young boy was walking down the street with his mother, who was Christmas shopping. She suddenly realized that he was no longer holding her hand. She turned around to look for him and saw him with his nose pressed against a store window looking at a manger scene. She rushed back, grabbed his hand and pulled him toward her. "Look, mother," he exclaimed, "look at baby Jesus. There is baby Jesus in the hay." "Come on, son," she said impatiently, "We don't have time for that!" And off they went.

We know that feeling, don't we? We are so busy buying gifts, cooking, decorating, wrapping, and going that we don't have time for Jesus. Slow down enough to realize the real significance of Christmas. In this Christmas season take time to reach out and help somebody who has a deep need. Take time to visit someone who is sick, shut-in, or lonely at Christmas. Take time to listen to your children, husband, or wife. Find a few moments of quiet and let the spirit of God settle upon you. Maybe that moment is right now as you come to the Lord's table.

Distraction

There is another mood that people sometimes have at Christmastime. This is the mood of being distracted. We are simply preoccupied with other things. The innkeeper in the Christmas story is an example of this mood. I don't believe that the innkeeper was hostile toward Mary or Joseph. He simply didn't have room in his inn for them. Other folks had crowded them out. At Christmastime, we sometimes let everything else crowd out the authentic meaning of Christmas.

The Courier-Journal, the Louisville, Kentucky newspaper, had an article on Ginny Wiseheart, who had worked for twenty-one years in Stewart's Department Store wrapping Christmas gifts. "Most customers are very nice, but just about now, this time of year, people start getting irritable," she said. "Maybe they don't like your wrap or they have to wait too long. We get those little plastic number cards thrown at us. I almost got hit in the head with one." This attitude of hostility is reflected in the words of the store clerk who watched customers nudging each other, stepping on toes, and pushing as they tried to get to the sales table. "Thank God, Christmas comes only once a year!"

We become so preoccupied with shopping, traveling, decorating, and buying gifts that we forget that all of these things should point us to the Christ whose birth we celebrate. Here in the quietness of these moments at the Lord's table, focus your heart and mind on the central figure we worship at Christmas — Christ.

Getting in the Mood for Christmas

I heard about a woman who called up her minister and complained about the music which had been selected for the outdoor service. She wanted some Christmas carols sung at the lighting of the Christmas tree, but she complained: "I don't understand it. All of these Christmas songs are so distressingly theological." "But madam, after all," he replied, "Christmas was a theological affair." For persons like this, they seldom realize themselves that an attitude of secularism seems to lie beneath the surface of their thinking.

It is so easy with all the commercialism, rushing, busyness, impatience, cynicism and many other distractions to find it difficult to get in the right mood for Christmas. Christmas can become distorted, and we may forget part of the tradition. We may find ourselves falling into the wrong emphasis. But, if somehow we can still remember to tell the tale of deliverance about how God has come uniquely in the birth of Jesus Christ, then maybe we are in the real mood for Christmas. Maybe cynicism can be transformed into hope, impatience into patience, busyness and rushing into quiet and peace, and commercialism into celebration and joy. Let's get in the right mood as we come to the Lord's table.

Finding the Mood

The mood of Christmas can be expressed in several ways. Christmas is a time of remembering ... remembering those childhood hours of merriment with family and friends around the tree and table. Remembering stories about angels, the Bethlehem inn, the cattle stall, and the birth of a baby, a star, wise men, and a manger crib. Christmas is a time of hearing...hearing greetings of "Merry Christmas," and "Peace on Earth." Hearing familiar carols...Handel's "Hallelujah Chorus" and Vivaldi's "Gloria." Christmas is also a time of giving... giving gifts to those we love. Giving with a new insight, as Emerson phrased it, "The only real gift is a portion of ourselves." Giving, as Jesus did, to the poor, the lonely, the needy. Christmas is also a time of receiving... receiving the gift of God's Son, aware that as many as receive him to them he gives power to become the sons and daughters of God...receiving the wonder and beauty and mystery of the gift of God's presence.

Christmas is a time of hoping... Hoping for a world filled with peace, good will, tolerance, compassion, and understanding...Hoping that in the midst of darkness and difficulties for the assurance of the abiding presence of God. Christmas is a time of loving...loving by shedding our inhibitions enough to care...loving by touching, noticing, remembering, listening, understanding, and embracing. Christmas is a time of birthing ... birthing from the old to the new...from staleness to freshness... good to the better, the better to the best, and the lowest to the highest. Birthing in the words of Thomas Merton where "Christ, light of light, is born today, and since He is born to us, He is born in us, and, therefore, we also are born today. That is to say, our souls are born to new life and new light, by receiving him who is the Truth." Christmas is a time of thanking. Thanking those who have helped us and loved us along the way. And thanking God for his great love. Christmas is a time of worshipping ... worshipping by falling down before the Christ and declaring that he is Lord of Lords and King of kings.

Are you in the mood for Christmas? You can choose your mood. You can choose to hold onto your difficulties or joys, failures or hopes, problems or dreams. You make the choice. No matter what circumstances you may find yourself in, you can choose your mood. You may not be able to control your circumstances, but you can control your response to your situation. I choose to let my mood for Christmas be one of worshipfulness and adoration. I hope you will also choose that mood. What will be your response to this Child called Jesus? Come now and let us commune at the Lord's table on this Christmas Eve.

O Divine Redeemer, we celebrate the coming of Christ into the world on this Christmas Eve. We open our hearts that he might be born anew within us. May his coming enable us to live and to love as you would have us do. May the Living Bread and the one whose blood was shed nourish us at his table. In the name of the Emmanuel we pray. Amen.

12. The Abiding Presence

PSALM 90:1-12
MATTHEW 28:1-10

Howard Lowery, who was at one time president of Wooster College, entertained Desmond MacCarthy, the drama critic for *the London Sunday Times*, by taking him to see a play on Broadway one night. After the play, they came out into the dark night and they were almost blinded by all the lights and splendor of Broadway. The drama critic turned and asked: "Tell me how do you Americans ever manage to celebrate anything?"

How Do We Celebrate the Resurrection?

How in the world do we celebrate the reality of the living Christ with the way we Americans celebrate everything else? Everything we do always seems so spectacular. Everything from soap to jeans is made to look phenomenal. A rock singer comes to town and we have to bring in the state troopers to keep the teenagers under control. At basketball games, fights break out and players and the crowd sometimes go wild. Thousands fill stadiums to watch football games. A movie star comes to town and people will turn out by the hundreds and thousands to get a glimpse of him or her. How do we celebrate something like the resurrection of Jesus Christ when we go to such extremes for all kinds of other things of much less importance?

Well, we have to admit that we celebrate it in a much more modest and tame sort of approach than some of these other events. We come to the communion table today, nevertheless, and we have placed it in the center of our service to emphasize that this is one of the central events within the worship of the Christian Church. When we gather at the Lord's table, it is not an addendum to worship. It is at the very center of our worship today, because we are seeking to proclaim that Jesus Christ is a living Lord who meets us in our worship in this hour.

In the passage of scripture which we read today, some women went to the tomb to anoint the body of Jesus. When they arrived at the tomb, they did not find a dead body to be anointed, but a Lord who had risen. There are some lessons in this biblical story for us on how to celebrate the presence of the living Christ today.

Believe in the Risen Christ

One of the messages which they were told on that significant day was that they should believe in the risen Christ. Now that is difficult when you ponder it for a moment. The Old Testament Psalm reminds us that God is from everlasting to everlasting. But man/woman is only here for a short while - sixty to seventy years, and then he/she is gone. We acknowledge our mortality and we affirm the eternity of God. We wrestle with how to deal with the shortness of our life and the everlastingness of God. But the angel announced the aliveness of our Lord, and Christ himself told them to believe in his resurrection. His resurrection also tells us something about our own "everlastingness." But this is not easy to grasp.

The New Testament relates the resurrection appearances of Jesus, although we are not sure of their exact order. Jesus appeared first to Mary Magdalene at the tomb, then to the other women as they left the tomb, most likely Peter was next, then the ten disciples as they gathered together in Jerusalem, the eleven with Thomas present, the seven by the Sea of Tiberias, the eleven in Galilee, the two on the road to Emmaus. Later he appeared to James, then he appeared to five hundred, to all the disciples again, and then later to Paul. The resurrection of Jesus Christ is the foundation stone of the New Testament. His resurrection affirms his life and teachings. Because he lives, we shall live also. We often sing on Easter Sunday the hymn, "He Lives." But we need to celebrate his living presence at times other than Easter. We have celebrated at this table today not simply a memory about a Christ who lived in the past, and who is dead and gone now, but we have affirmed today that Christ is a living presence with us.

A Real Presence

Is he real? We acknowledge that the bread was real. We acknowledge that the cup was real. We can taste, touch, see, eat or drink them. But is Christ real? What is reality? In the *Revised Standard Version,* John 1:17 reads, "Grace and truth came through Jesus Christ." The word for truth is translated by James Moffatt as "reality." "Grace and *reality* came through Jesus Christ." Jesus Christ has come as the reality of God among us. For us, he represented the real, authentic presence of God in our world, and he is still real with us today. We do not focus just on a memory. We have not come to this table merely to reflect, to think, and be thankful. We gather to celebrate that Jesus Christ is a living Lord with us. We commune not with a memory but with the real presence of Christ who is here with us. He is not a presence in the elements. That is not my point. The elements are symbolic of the real Christ who is here with us in our lives.

You and I can see the chairs sitting by the pulpit. The chairs are beside the pulpit. A chair may be near the pulpit. It may be beside the pulpit, but a chair is not really "with" the pulpit. Only a person can have presence. When we say Jesus Christ is with us, we are affirming a vital, real relationship with us in our lives and within the world. He is a living presence and continues to work his redemption in and through his church. And you and I are a part of that church.

A Muslim was talking one day to a Christian missionary and said, "I feel sorry for you Christians. We can go to Mecca and see the grave of our great leader. But you can go to Jerusalem and you cannot find the grave or the body of your founder." Now you can imagine what the missionary must have told him. Isn't that the very key to our faith? We do not have a grave where we can go and find the body of Christ, because he is a living Lord still present among us. I like the way George Buttrick expressed it when he said: "The symbol of the Christian faith is not an hourglass or a grave, but an empty cross and an empty grave - and bread from living seed, with wine from living vines. Perhaps we should say that Christianity has no fixed or absolute symbol: It has a presence."[15] This is a living presence which the Christian faith affirms. It is the abiding presence of Christ.

Rejoice in the Resurrection

Notice also that we read in this Scripture passage that when the women meet the angel and Christ, they are told to rejoice. Isn't it interesting that at the birth of Christ, angels told the shepherds that they brought them "tidings of great joy?" We read that the women were awestruck,

15 George A. Buttrick, *The Interpreter's Bible*, (Nashville: Abingdon Press, 1951). Vol. 7, 576.

but they were also filled with joy. They are told by the angel not to be afraid. The greeting which Christ spoke to Mary was the traditional greeting of that day, but literally in Greek it means "rejoice." They were told: "Rejoice, Christ lives." We continue to affirm, "He is risen." He is a living Lord among us today. That should fill our lives with great joy as we gather at his table to celebrate his resurrection. With the reality of his presence in our lives, let us go forth into the world to live as his children.

Sometimes I think our problem in celebrating the resurrection of Christ is like what Annie Dillard wrote when she was describing grace as a waterfall.[16] We stand under the waterfall trying to fill up our cup from its overabundance. But one cannot fill up a cup any more when it is already full. Some of us have stood under numerous water falls of life, and our cups are full of all kinds of ingredients. Sometimes we cannot let the cup of our life be filled with the presence of God until we have emptied it of less important matters. Our cups are too filled with the world, and until some of the world is emptied from it, Christ cannot fill our lives with the power of his living presence. Let us then stand under the waterfall of the grace of God. Lift up our cups and let him fill us to the brim and to overflowing. Again and again.

Share the Good News of Resurrection

In this story we also observe that the angel instructed the women to "Go and share the message of the risen Christ with his disciples." Having seen the Christ, they are aware that he is a living God. They are told to go and share this great truth with others. We are never called just to receive the good news about the risen Christ. Those

---

16 Quoted in John Killinger, *The Cup and The Waterfall* (New York: Paulist Press, 1983), 2.

who have been reconciled by Christ are now commissioned to be agents of reconciliation in the world. Those of us who have experienced the power of the redemptive grace of the living presence, should go joyfully to share this great good news with other people.

The New Testament is filled with Christ coming into the lives of people and changing them for the good. A woman is caught in the very act of adultery, and Jesus forgives her and she begins life again. He went to the home of Zacchaeus, a sinner. Zacchaeus is forgiven, and he begins his life anew. Even a thief, when he is dying on a cross beside Jesus, received forgiveness from Christ for his sins and the assurance of life beyond. Just as he came into the lives of persons in the past, Jesus comes into your life and my life, and he offers us the opportunity to begin life anew - to experience forgiveness - to let our lives be filled with his presence which offers authentic life.

Worship the Living Lord

Our text also tells us that when the women met the living Christ, they fell down and worshipped him. In him, they experienced the reality of God. Jesus Christ has opened for us the avenue of communion with the Father. Through Christ, we experience the worship of a God who is both real and personal. I don't know when you first recall worshipping God. I mean *really* worshipping God. I am not referring to the time you first remember going to church or Sunday School, but do you recall that moment in your life when God really reached down and got hold of your life and you felt the power of his living presence? I remember an experience I had as a teenager of fifteen. I had been going to church for some months and had been struggling with my own relationship with God and life.

I would usually walk about a mile from my home to my church, and on one particular Sunday afternoon as I was walking to church, I felt an overwhelming sense of the power of the presence of God in my life, and I knew that it would never be the same again. God had become real to me.

I can remember the years which I spent working in scout camps where I would rise early and go down by the lake and mountainside, and reflect prayerfully. There I encountered the Spirit of God. I can remember meeting God in quietness while sitting in church, and in the quietness around our family table at mealtime, or at Christmas or Thanksgiving. I have sensed God while I was present in a hospital holding the hand of a dying man who looked up at me and said: "Pastor, I am really not afraid to die. I have peace." While sitting in church feeling my own sense of grief, I have experienced the presence of God in that moment as he communicated grace to me. I have been with some of you in this congregation at times which were difficult and have sensed the strength that you have found from the abiding presence of God. Each of us in his or her way needs to meet the Christ who appears on your Emmaus Road. He comes along your path of life to assure you of his continued presence.

They Sang a Hymn

When the disciples finished observing the Lord's Supper, we read that they sang a hymn. Most likely the hymn was the great *Hallel*. This hymn may have been Psalms 136. Jesus, as the rabbi, may have quoted the first part of the hymn and the disciples most likely concluded by quoting the second part of each verse. When Jesus finished the first part, they would have responded: "For his steadfast love endures forever." They affirmed their belief that "from generation to generation, and from everlasting to everlasting there is God." He is always here. He endures forever! We have come in his presence today at this table to acknowledge the liveliness, the eternity, and the abiding presence of the God who is here with us now in life.

John Masefield, in a very moving drama entitled *The Everlasting Mercy*, pictures a Roman Centurion who brings a message to Pilate informing him that Jesus has been crucified, but that his body is not in the grave. Procula, the wife of Pilate, turned to the Centurion and asked, "Do you think he is dead?" "No, lady, I don't," the centurion replied. "Then, where is he?" she asked. The Centurion responded, "Let loose in the world, lady."[17] And so he is!

By the resurrection of Christ, God's spirit has been set loose in the world, and it is an abiding presence with us. Feed and feast upon it. Leave this day with the assurance that we live not alone, but with the power of the eternal God of the universe in our lives this day and with us forever.

God of Eternity, we have come to feed upon your Spirit today. We thank You for feeding us. May we now go forth to feed others, as we have experienced Your abiding presence. Amen.

---

[17] John Masefield, *The Everlasting Mercy* (London: Sidgwick and Jackson, Ltd., 1911), 77f.

www.ingramcontent.com/pod-product-compliance
Lightning Source LLC
Chambersburg PA
CBHW071729090426
42738CB00011B/2431